Norse-Gaelic PAGANISM

"*Norse-Gaelic Paganism* is a fascinating look at the crossover between two related but distinct cultures. Humphrey painstakingly details the history, beliefs, and intersection of Norse and Celtic peoples and offers an approach to modern practice that blends the two. Truly essential reading for anyone interested in this often-overlooked history, anyone curious about how the cultures might have influenced each other, and, of course, anyone who seeks to combine them within their own spiritual practices. A perfect addition to any library."

MORGAN DAIMLER, AUTHOR OF *PAGAN PORTALS: GODS AND GODDESSES OF IRELAND*, *PANTHEON: THE NORSE*, AND *PANTHEON: THE IRISH*

"Reading this book was like taking a tour of my hometown with someone who knew secrets and history that I could only dream of knowing. Annie Cúglas Humphrey is that guide, and this book is a combination of a lodestone pointing us home and a giant, yellow circle on a map that says, 'you are here.'"

ERIKA WREN, HOST OF THE *THAT PAGAN MOM* PODCAST

Norse-Gaelic PAGANISM

VIKING AND IRISH MYTH AND MAGIC

ANNIE CÚGLAS HUMPHREY, PhD

Inner Traditions
Rochester, Vermont

Inner Traditions
One Park Street
Rochester, Vermont 05767
www.InnerTraditions.com

Cataloging-in-Publication Data for this title is available from the Library of Congress

ISBN 979-8-88850-255-6 (print)
ISBN 979-8-88850-256-3 (ebook)

Printed and bound in the United States by Lake Book Manufacturing, LLC

10 9 8 7 6 5 4 3 2

Text design and layout by Debbie Glogover
This book was typeset in Garamond Premier Pro with Gill Sans MT Pro, Le Monde Livre Cla Std, Parochus, and Soleil used as display typefaces

To send correspondence to the author of this book, mail a first-class letter to the author c/o Inner Traditions, One Park Street, Rochester, VT 05767, and we will forward the communication, or contact the author directly at **anniechumphrey.com**.

Contents

Acknowledgments

D'Artúr agus do Ruadhán,
mo bhéar agus mo mhús, le ghrá

Portions of the research of this book were completed while resident at Rutgers University in New Jersey, on Munsee Lenape ancestral land; and at the University of Connecticut, on Mohegan, Nipmunc, and Mashantucket Pequot ancestral land. I intend to pay respect to Indigenous people—past, present, and future—and honor those that have been historically and systemically disenfranchised. I also acknowledge that Rutgers University and the University of Connecticut, like the states of New Jersey and Connecticut, and the United States as a nation, were founded upon the exclusions and erasures of Indigenous peoples.

Additionally, portions of the research of this book were completed while funded by a Government of Ireland Postgraduate Studentship, granted by the Irish Research Council, at Trinity College Dublin in the Republic of Ireland.

This book would not have been possible without the camaraderie and support of dozens of people over the years. It is impossible to list them without imbuing a sense of hierarchy, for which I am sorrowful, and beg forgiveness! Endless thanks to: my beloved kinsmen Mat B, Ragnar, Kevin, Cory, Mike R, Josh, and Kaila. My fellow Northeast Thing committee members, including Sara P, Kat, Dave, Sarah C, Phish, Jen, Patty, Mike S, Freyjadis, Kurt, Nikki, John, and Chey. My Trinity colleagues Mat C, D.J., Chel, Jeremy, and Sandy. Friends near and far: Liz, Cameron, Stuart, Jad, Kerry, Garth, Justin, Autumn, and Martin. And last but nowhere near least, my daily support team of fellow heathen parents and creators, Erika Wren and Ristandi. *Takk fyrir!*

INTRODUCTION

The Whole from Its Parts

Annals written by Irish clerics report that in the year 858:

> . . . it was worth coming in order to kill those *Gall-Gaedil* ["Foreign Gaels"] who were slain there, for they were men who had forsaken their baptism, and they used to be called Norsemen, for they had the customs of the Norse, and had been fostered by them, and though the original Norsemen were evil to the churches, these were much worse, these people, wherever in Ireland they were.[1]

These "Foreign Gaels" appear here and in several other monastic records from the ninth century. They were treated with scorn and disgust by the writers, themselves Irish-language (*Gaeilge*) speakers, who were horrified by the actions of their fellow countrymen. These Gall-Gaedil had thrown in their lot with the Norse-speaking Vikings, who had first arrived in Ireland in the final years of the eighth century. For the cleric recording their activities, the Foreign Gaels were reprehensible for not only behaving like Norsemen, but also because doing so required them to refute their Christianity.[2]

This short passage reveals several historical facts. The first is that the gulf between "native" Gael and "foreign" Norse was not impossible to traverse. The second is that this cross-cultural exchange began quickly: the Norse trading town of *Dyflin* (later Dublin, the subject of chapter 1) was only settled in the year 841, less than a generation before the annalistic entry above. The third and most useful for this book is that while religion was among the differences between the Gaels and the Norse, that attribute was also possible to change.

Much ink has been spilled regarding the conversion of the Norse in Ireland to Christianity.* This is both as its own process, as well as part of the larger narrative of the Christianization of northern Europe. But historical, archeological, place-name, and folkloric evidence support both the spread of Norse pre-Christian religious practices into Ireland, as well as the mingling of Irish religious traditions rooted in the pre-Christian period. This fusion of two separate but related northern European cultures was carried across the North Atlantic, from southern Ireland to the Orkney Islands to Iceland, wherever Norse and Gaelic populations settled together. And while eventually these lands were fully integrated into the Christendom that characterized the European Middle Ages, for generations people lived these traditions. Their mark has been left on documents, artifacts, and tales. And because of these chance survivals, it is possible to contemplate, revive, and occupy the Norse-Gaelic worldview in modern times.

This book is the culmination of two decades' worth of curi-

*For instance, see Abrams's "The Conversion of the Scandinavians of Dublin" and "Conversion and the Church in Viking-Age Ireland," and Downham's "Religious and Cultural Boundaries between Vikings and Irish."

osity and labor. I do not intend it as the final word on the topic, but rather as the beginning of a conversation I hope continues long after my lifetime. After years of solitary practice, when I encountered the larger modern polytheist or "neo-pagan" community in the mid-2000s, I was surprised to find a strict boundary. Those who honored the gods of Ireland and other Celtic-family language regions often used the term "druid" to describe themselves, while those who followed Norse and other Germanic-family language traditions distinguished themselves as "heathen." There was a pervasive sense of division, often on gendered lines: druid organizations were frequently women-centered and prized magic and mysticism, while heathen groups were typically led by men and prided themselves on celebrating the practical rather than the arcane.

I wanted to respect the community as it existed, but I also felt uneasy navigating what seemed like an unnecessary separation. What seemed to others like a clear distinction between unrelated cultures appeared to me as an exciting chirality that generated dynamism and power by its near differences, like a lithium-ion battery. I had the opportunity to move to Ireland for a year-long Irish Studies program at University College Cork in 2007, and went with an open mind to learn as much as I could about the Irish end of my faith. Instead, I found even more evidence for the interplay and integration of "Germanic" and "Celtic" society in the form of the Vikings in Ireland and their descendants, the Hiberno-Norse.

When my now-husband and I visited the Isle of Man on spring break, we finally found the whole we had sought from its parts: a single island nation that fully acknowledged its roots from both Gaelic and Norse cultures. It manifests in amusing ways. One restaurant named their largest steak the "Manannán," and the second largest the "Odin." We visited as many local museums and bought as many volumes on Manx history as we could. In one, A. W. Moore's *The Folk-Lore of the Isle of Man*, Midsummer is described: ". . . this was the day on which the *Druadh* [Druids] cut the mistletoe, and thus enabled Balder to be slain."[3] Here we had found the seed we did not know we were looking for, the singular particulate around which condensed a new way of thinking for us. This was an explicit link between the Celtic druids and the Germanic god Balder (Old Icelandic *Baldr*), written out plainly at the end of the nineteenth century.*

When I returned to the United States to finish my undergraduate history degree, I managed two competing motivations. The first was to continue to explore and test documents and artifacts from the spaces where Norse and Gael had lived together to see if further evidence for their cultural fusion could be found. The second was to remain objective, open, and honest about the process. The best histories are those which question a small number of primary sources, sometimes even just one, and report back fairly and critically on what was found. I did not want to "cherry-pick" the finest examples out of context and spin them into a narrative that could easily be criticized as a self-fulfilling conclusion fabricated out of thrown-together data.

Rather, I began the long but rewarding process of studying medieval literature in its contemporary setting, being careful to contextualize and situate every narrative, figure, visual, and reference with the environment in which it was composed. I wrote a thesis on the appearance of Gaels in Icelandic settlement texts, the conclusions of which appear in the chapter on Iceland. I studied later medieval and

*Admittedly, Moore was likely participating in the contemporary preoccupation with equating *all* mythologies worldwide, making this an erroneous assertion, but the spark was lit regardless!

early modern narratives that repeat earlier themes and suggest oracular transmission of tales of Norse-Gaelic paganism. Finally, for my doctoral thesis, I returned to Ireland—this time to Trinity College at the University of Dublin, that Hiberno-Norse town *par excellence.* There, I researched and analyzed a trio of Middle Irish dynastic propaganda texts for how they remembered the Norse in Ireland. The summary of that dissertation is found in chapter six.

I collate these discoveries in this book to allow other readers, historians, modern polytheists, and curious seekers to read my conclusions and form their own. While the final chapter includes some material that can be used to recreate Norse-Gaelic pagan practices for a modern mindset, this book as a whole is not meant as an irrefutable instruction manual or dogmatic declaration of what once was. It is a guidebook to a vanished country. I present you these glimpses and waypoints in the hope that you venture there on your own, and the historical material becomes for you what you will.

TERMINOLOGY USED IN THIS BOOK

Names have a power and magic all their own. Inevitably, they fall short of describing exactly what they are supposed to. To give something a name references ideas that are not meant to be included, and excludes some that ought to be involved. This problem multiplies exponentially when using modern terms for medieval ideas—or medieval terms for modern ones. The best we can do is talk about them explicitly so that their use in the book is best understood by any reader, regardless of their background knowledge or previous understanding of the terms. This is not meant to change all use of these names in all places, but rather to let you know how I am working with them here.

Celt/Celtic: First written in Greek over 2,500 years ago, this term refers broadly to people who use a language from the vast Celtic family. Previous members of this group were found in western and central Europe. Today the Celtic languages are found in two subgroups in the extreme northwest: Brittonic Celtic, which includes Welsh, Breton, and Cornish; and Goidelic Celtic, which includes Irish, Scottish Gaelic, and Manx. The relationship between ethnic/genetic ancestry and the use of the language is complicated. The term "Celtic" was picked up, after extremely long disuse, in the modern period for racial and nationalistic ends. In this book, "Celtic" refers exclusively to the broader language family.

Gael/Gaelic: This refers to people who use one of the languages in the Goidelic language family, descended from *Goídelc* or Old Irish, which was spoken nearly without dialect across what is now Ireland, the Isle of Man, and western Scotland. In the ninth through twelfth centuries, this term was spelled as *Gaidheal* and many other variants, and was used extensively in the primary sources looked at in this book. There are other contemporary ethnic terms such as *Féni* and *Cruithin*,[4] but "Gael" is used most consistently. It is a useful term to refer to *Goídelc*-speakers wherever they were, as it sidesteps both medieval and modern political boundaries.

Germanic: A language family that includes modern English, Dutch, Swedish, and Icelandic, and medieval languages such as Old Norse and Old Saxon. This term is loaded by modern racist ideology, and is used solely in this book to refer to related languages and the cultures that used them in the ninth through twelfth centuries.

Heathen/Heathenism: From Old English *hǣþen* (pronounced "hahthen") and possibly of further antiquity. A calque or direct translation of the Latin *pāgānus* (see "Pagan" below), referring to non-Christians, especially those found outside of cities or other community areas served by Christian churches. By using a specifically non-Latinate term, the word is used as an adjective label to describe religious practices and spiritual beliefs in a Germanic context, particularly but not exclusively by speakers of Old Norse. This book uses this label as an umbrella term for Norse devotional and magical practices of the ninth through twelfth centuries, but this does not imply that such things were all the same everywhere. "Heathen" is also used by modern religious practitioners, including the author themself, but this is an intentionally anachronistic label of reclamation.

Irish: Of or pertaining to the geographical island of Ireland. As today, Ireland in the ninth through twelfth centuries was inhabited by occupants speaking both Gaelic and Germanic languages, and this book is careful to **not** equate Gaelic speakers with residents of Ireland. A tenth-century permanent resident of Dyflin, for instance, was Irish, even if their family background and only language was Norse.

Norse: Short for Old Norse, known to its own speakers as *dǫnsk tunga* or "the tongue of the *Danir*,"[5] spoken in the ninth through twelfth centuries across Europe, into eastern Asia and northern Africa, and at the North American settlements in what is now Greenland and Newfoundland. Gaelic primary sources refer to several subsets, such as Danair and *Lochlannaigh*,* and they use terms for them like *geinti* (gentile, that is, non-Christian or pagan) and gall (foreigner); the use of these labels is covered further in chapter 2.

*Throughout this book, different forms of this Old/Middle Irish term are used: *Lochlannaig(h)* is the nominative plural, while *Lochlannach* is the nominative singular. The adjective and genitive forms switch: *Lochlannaigh* ("of [a] Viking") and *Lochlannach* ("of Vikings").

Norse is used in this book as a catch-all for people using Old Norse language and cultural values such as trading towns and ship technology. A sub-term is "Hiberno-Norse," a resident of a Norse town in Ireland. (*Hibernia* is a Latin name for Ireland and thus used here as an adjective.)

Pagan/Paganism: An umbrella term from the Latin pāgānus, meaning either "rustic," as in not a city-dweller, or possibly "civilian," as in not a soldier, that is, untrained; in the later centuries of the Christianized Roman Empire the term was used to describe non-Christians and their practices. Prior to dogmatic, exclusive monotheism, there was no need for a description of religious worship and philosophy outside of other ethnic determinants. This book uses this term to categorize polytheistic (belief in multiple gods) and/or animist (belief in divinity in multiple, concurrent sources) religious activity, found in pre- and non-Christian contexts.

Viking: A term for sea-going Norse raiders who struck against coastal and riverine settlements from the end of the late eighth century onwards. While the name is meant for the raiders specifically (and most of them had other occupations besides), their predations made enough of an impression on contemporary chroniclers that the entire time period is often called "the Viking Age." This results in "Viking" serving as an adjective for Norse culture and artifacts, even those unrelated to raiding, such as "Viking houses" or "Viking towns." "Viking" is also a very popular term today, and while most people now know that Vikings did not wear horned helmets or furred loincloths, the image of a seagoing raider summons a mountain of correspondences, for better or worse. Because of this, I restrict use of "Viking" in this book to refer exclusively to the raiders, and therefore it does not come up as often as one may expect in a volume about the Norse.

NORSE-GAELS IN HISTORY, AND HISTORICAL WRITING

It is apparent the entire premise of writing about medieval history is fraught with pre-conceptions and erroneous connections. Further complicating the issue, and perhaps the reason why this book does not have much in the way of antecedents, is that historians and medievalists need to focus on one subfield to do the sort of research that completes a doctorate and produces peer-reviewed literature. Old Norse scholarship, often specifically Old Icelandic, requires one set of linguistic tools and specialized training that can take years to acquire. Old and Middle Irish require another.

Even when one academic learns both, their ability to discuss and publish is curtailed by conferences and journals that are managed by experts of a singular subfield. While it is not unpleasant to be the resident Norse expert at Irish colloquia and the Irish specialist in Norse research fora, it is somewhat lonely. This is likely a product of the Anglophone world's inherent bias toward English history, where Middle Irish, Old Norse, and other medieval languages are valued by their proximity to Old and Middle English. While I am all for acknowledging and studying as many contemporary societies as possible, the English relationship to Norse and Gaelic cultural interchange is not a priority here!

Nonetheless, this is not empty territory. The high-water mark of recent scholarship is the four-way collaboration between Colmán Etchingham, Jón Viðar Sigurðsson, Máire Ní Mhaonaigh, and Elizabeth Ashman Rowe entitled *Norse-Gaelic Contacts in a Viking World*, published by Brepols in 2019. Gísli Sigurðsson* has

*No relation to Jón Viðar; Icelandic last names are generally patronymics rather than family names. First name(s) are used rather than last names.

also produced work on Gaelic themes in Norse literature, notably 1988's *Gaelic Influence in Iceland: Historical and Literary Contacts.* The small volume goes in and out of print, a testament both to the enduring interest in Irish and Icelandic medieval history as well as its perennial obscurity. Other books inherently touch on Norse and Gaelic themes in their discussion of Irish Sea-area history, such as Ben Hudson's *Viking Pirates and Christian Princes* (2005), Clare Downham's *Viking Kings of Britain and Ireland* (2007), Mary Valante's *The Vikings in Ireland* (2008), David Griffith's *Vikings of the Irish Sea* (2010), and the 2018 collaboration between Howard B. Clarke, Sheila Dooley, and Ruth Johnson: *Dublin and the Viking World.*

This particular book beholds the *what, when*, and *how* that historians and archeologists have labored to answer, values and upholds their contributions, and then asks *why*? Why did Norse people moving west in the very late eighth and ninth centuries set up towns in Ireland, intermarry with elites and commoners, learn the Irish language, and raise their children in their new homelands?

Why did the Gaels in Ireland, Scotland, and the islands in between themselves learn Norse shipbuilding and sailing technology, use their currency, intermarry, move to towns, and become members of the larger Norse-speaking world from the Gaelic-speaking one? Why did this fusion of cultures travel further across the Atlantic to the Faroes, Iceland, Greenland, and beyond? Why did their stories, mythologies, fables, and beliefs become intertwined, and remembered long after the whole of northern Europe became Christianized? And why is the cultural heritage of the Norse-Gaels so compelling today?

These questions, while clearly focused on a particular region and time period, are also relevant outside the medieval North Atlantic. Much of twentieth and twenty-first century historical scholarship is on *colonialism* and its products, such as decolonialization and post-colonial theory. Premodern history, such as that in this book's purview, offers a look at pre- or rather "a-colonial" cultural interchange. How do societies that are not interested in empire-building and do not have the mechanisms for sustained foreign resource extraction interact with other societies of this type? Fascinating and careful interchanges occur anywhere neither side has the might of a modern empire behind them.

While the Norse were not quite in Ireland for a picnic, and their ready participation in the slave trade is acknowledged, they also were not operating as members of a well-funded and technologically advanced state seeking wealth to bring home to their "mother" nation. Simply put, Gael and Norse were both peoples who functioned without modern coercion or cultural superiority maxims motivating their movement. They looked to the other culture and saw ideals and structures they could admire, and as this book demonstrates, they took what they liked and made it their own.

Indeed, the act of coming from elsewhere could grant something or someone even further prestige. For instance, in *Laxdæla Saga*, the Icelander Egill Skallagrímsson proclaims of a boy born to an enslaved Irish noblewoman and an Icelandic father: "He's of even better family on his mother's side than his father's."[6] As covered in chapter 4, the contemporary accuracy of the Icelandic sagas and other medieval literature is suspect—without voice recorders, there is no way to know that Egill said these exact words—but this supports the *idea* of a leading Icelander recognizing and complimenting Irish dynastic status. Class superseded ethnolinguistic boundaries.

For decades, going on centuries, study on documents concerning the history of the North Atlantic assumed that Norse and Gael saw each other as enemies, or at the very least, irredeemable outsiders. Genealogies, poetry, historical narratives, and other comparable literature for the most part have been analyzed by experts in *either* Old Norse or Middle Irish, leaving the experiences and conceptions of speakers of the other language to scholars in that subfield. The very act of modern research is thus conditioned to find Norse and Gael in opposition. This makes the many moments collected in this book where Norse and Gaelic ideology align all the more precious, and thought-provoking.

THE LANGUAGE(S) OF NORSE-GAELIC STUDY

There are multiple languages under purview in this book, as well as varying medieval and modern forms of them. For instance, as already shown, Old Norse (Old Icelandic) *Baldr* becomes *Baldur* in modern Icelandic, while *Gaedhil* in Middle Irish becomes *Gael* in Modern Irish. It could easily be argued that other descendent languages, such as modern Danish and modern Manx, respectively, have equal claim to the "correct" modern form of the medieval term. This usually shows up in scholarship based on the author's native country and/or area of training. As I am from the northeastern United States and did my PhD in Ireland, I surely have linguistic bias toward both American and Irish style spelling and word choice that is invisible to me but apparent to, say, a reader from Canada or Singapore.

So, which spelling should be used when talking about medieval people and places, in a different modern language? I admit distaste for outright Anglicizations, such as the magnificent Middle Irish name *Muircheartach* (*Myrkjartan* in Old Norse) becoming the anemic "Murtagh" in English. It could help an English reader to translate names between Middle Irish and Old Norse, however; some are self-evident (*Níall* and *Njáll*, *Cormac* and *Kormákr*), while some require a bit of squinting to see as the same name (*Gormlaith* and *Kormlöð*, *Donnchad* and *Dungaðr*). For the most part I use the name as it is used in the document under question, but may reiterate the name as it appears elsewhere to remind the reader. Keeping the name as it appears in the source also contextualizes it, in case future scholarship or discoveries find that there were two or more people with similar names.

The Icelandic characters Þ/þ ("Thorn") and Ð/ð ("Eth") both render "th" sounds and are usually put into English as "th" and "dh," respectively. Modern Icelandic pronounces actual "th" as a "t" sound (the beer named *Thule* is pronounced like "Toola," for instance), so this is less than ideal. I use þ and ð whenever possible in this book. There are also some vowel sounds like *ei* and *æ* that are pronounced differently from what English speakers may expect. I highly recommend those interested to find multimedia resources on Icelandic and learn how to say these names correctly.

Similarly, Irish language uses different pronunciation rules with the same Roman alphabet as English, which can lead to both frustration and ridicule that "Irish doesn't make sense." I remind those who feel this way that the historical Irish language was worked out in Latinate characters long before Old English was! It is gauche to declare Irish names like Tairdealbach ("TUR-lock") unpronounceable when we have names like Featherstonehaugh ("FERN-shaw") and Gloucester ("GLOSS-ter") in our midst. Irish is regular, though it does have a lengthy list of rules, and medieval and modern pronunciation varies somewhat. Again, there are plenty of resources in text, audio, and video format to pronounce Irish properly.

NORSE-GAELIC PAGANISM AND CONVERSION

The phenomenon of Norse heathen religion coming to Ireland and other Gaelic-speaking areas has only been treated in passing and mostly as a footnote, a curious eddy in the stream of time that invariably carried all residents of the European peninsula into a Christian worldview. Similarly, the 120 years between the settlement of Iceland and its official conversion to Christianity are typically considered a preamble to Icelandic Church history. The generations who lived during this period certainly did not consider themselves pre-Christians or at a lesser developmental stage.

Christian conversion narratives from early medieval western Europe are generally one-way: the ignorant and naïve are informed about Christianity and, with the lightest touch of narrative tension, eventually convert themselves and their descendants to Christian monotheism. Apostasy, the act of renouncing Christian baptism, is particularly dastardly because to do so subverts the literary theme that to learn about Christianity is to want to partake in it. Terminology for apostates uses verbs concerned with falling, slipping, sliding, or otherwise acting without care. To recant conversion is seen as a lack of uprighteousness and a moral failing, rather than an active mental decision or a change of heart.

In this light, the overarching conversion narrative of the Norse in Ireland has been straightforward and succinct. They came, they saw, they became involved in Gaelic dynasties and politics that reached across the Irish Sea and the English Channel, and they converted. The churches and bishops who were supported by the Hiberno-Norse have a rich documentation, which is natural for a religion that depends on literacy and relies on the written word for its legitimacy.

Left unrecorded, and thus unseen and unpreserved, was the flow of religious ideas and practices in the other direction: the spread, adaptation, and survival of the gods and myths of the Norsemen *into* Ireland, Scotland, and the Isles. The descendants of those Norse speakers would later take literacy to new heights in the form of Icelandic saga and historical literature, though this was done by a fully Christianized population who had a limited interest in, and perhaps a reduced ability to, record and perpetuate heathen concepts in writing (further explored in chapter 6). But the phenomenon of apostasy, intentionally going against one's Christian baptism, nonetheless existed. It was written down, such as in the form of the Gall-Gaedil referenced at the start of this chapter. It was ridiculed and condemned. Yet by the act of setting it in writing, it was documented for future generations.

We in the twenty-first century, living in societies that are verging on secular if not wholly atheist, now have the ability to pick up the pieces that were discarded so long ago. They will never reconstitute exactly the religion of the Norse-Gaels, as there is little to go on. In his introduction to Patricia Terry's translation of the *Elder Edda*, Charles Dunn wryly comments,

> It is difficult now to reconstruct Norse religion—as difficult, in fact, as if a latter-day archaeologist were forced to reconstruct Christianity from an excavation that yielded only a fourteenth-century crucifix, a piece of Victorian stained glass, and a twentieth-century Christmas-tree light.[7]

But more to the point, there was no *one* religion, then or now; customs varied from household to household, and from generation to generation, just as the shape of our collective holidays and celebrations today naturally alter in circumstances that inevitably change. Furthermore, if there was an alternate history of the European peninsula where Christianity or any other monotheistic dogmatic religion never took hold, the practices of the Norse-Gaels of a thousand years ago would differ dramatically from those of their spiritual descendants today.

Let us not eschew modern medicine, scientific principles, strides toward disability accommodations, or a hundred other advances made in the past millennium! Also, there is no need to fetishize the Viking Age in our clothing or habits, whether based on archeological artifacts or film studio visions; that era of conversion is merely the other end of the bridge.

Rather, let us behold the fragments that have survived to the twenty-first century, and ponder and honor them as revenants from a long-ago age. While their preservation was by chance, we can breathe new life into them as tools and symbols of a worldview worth reviving. Norse-Gaelic paganism is currently in pieces, but from and between these parts, we can glimpse and celebrate the whole.

1
Dyflin
Heathen Norse Dublin

Modern-day Dublin, capital of the Republic of Ireland, is a sprawling city spread north and south of the River Liffey on its way to the Irish Sea. The Liffey is met with Georgian-era canals and small named tributaries like the Dodder and Bradogue, which appear in narrow channels and disappear into underground culverts, and the rain and tides vary these river systems from muddy rivulets to brackish water that reaches the bottom of the bridges. Until very recently, few buildings exceeded five stories, and there are only a handful of noticeable hills in the greater Dublin area. It is a flattish, riverine city that is charming, relatively small, and notably wet.

It is also a city of two names, carried today on the linguistic divide between English and Irish, but bearing a long history that may itself predate the Norse. Dublin is also *Baile Átha Cliath*, the Town at the Ford (i.e., navigable river crossing) of the Reed Hurdles (intentionally sunk earthworks to create or maintain said ford). In modern Irish these syllables are run together, and it sounds like "Balla Cleeah" or even "Blocklee." Middle Irish still pronounced *th*, similarly to how it is spoken in English, so medieval residents would have called their town *Áth Cliath*, "Oth Cleeoth," although the final "th" is likely to have dropped on familiarity.

The precise site of Áth Cliath is unknown as central Dublin has undergone extensive rebuilding—if such reed hurdles or other settlement markers would have left much of a trace in the archeological record in the first place. But from context, it seems to have been around the modern suburb of Islandbridge, south of Phoenix Park and between the Irish National War Memorial Gardens and Heuston Station. Islandbridge today is packed with new construction apartment blocks, trendy shops, and young professionals and their families; an ever-renewing area of residence in Dublin.

Further downstream to the west, where the Poddle meets the Liffey, and currently the site of Dublin Castle's garden, was a deep-water "black pool" (*dubh linn*), which gives its name to Irish *Duiblinn*. The *b* (later *bh*) makes an "f" sound and was rendered into Old Norse as Dyflin. It is presumed that this deepwater confluence made an attractive port for Viking ships where they could be kept in the water ready for launching, but also close enough to shore to facilitate movement of goods and people on and off of them.

> Thus, while the *Annals of Ulster* report that the Vikings set up "a ship-camp at Duiblinn (*longport oc Duiblinn*)," just four years later they refer to the newcomers as "the foreigners of Áth Cliath (*Gallaibh Átha Cliath*)" indicating a confusion over, or indifference to, placenames even at this early stage . . .[1]

Just as modern Dublin is also "Blocklee," Dyflin, or Norse-speaking Dublin, was also Áth Cliath. For ease, in this book I will refer to Dyflin specifically to mean the settlement on the Liffey in the ninth through twelfth centuries. When the Cambro-Normans crossed the Irish Sea and set up a new outpost of their kingdom there, the town was still very aware of its position as a Norse town, in a world where Vikings had become well-paid mercenaries, established traders, church officials, and aristocratic administrators. The Dubliners of Norse descent—sometimes called Hiberno-Norse by modern scholars or, with a clatter of syllables, Hiberno-Scandinavians—called themselves *Ostmen*, Men (in the sense of "people") of the East, in reference to their position looking west towards the rest of the Norse-speaking world.

RELIGION IN DYFLIN

When the Norse settled in Ireland from the beginning of the ninth century onwards, they came from a region of Europe that had not previously been part of Roman imperial administration. As such, there was a lack of social institutions that were found in other areas on the Continent that had been maintained, if not by the Roman Church directly, then by local Christians in a desire to emulate and stay connected with the trade, status, wealth, and security that Christianity provided to medieval Europe after the Roman Empire. Far northern Europe, including today's Norway, Sweden, and Denmark, functioned in a social order described as "pre-Christian."

This is one of the most frustrating aspects of any attempt to study or understand heathenism: it was an oral culture for which recording theological or even legal material was alien. Unfortunately as it was a preliterate culture—indeed, one that prized memory and oral recitation—we have nothing clearly about heathenism that was written down by a heathen. Apart from a handful of quasi-magical runic carvings, all literature from Germanic northern Europe came firmly after conversion, from the hands of Christian authors.

However, the editorial weight of these writers varied, and we believe that we have fairly substantial hints at pre-Christian beliefs encoded in poetry, literature, and even law texts. We also have archaeology: objects from homes and workspaces, inhumations or burials, and sometimes entire landscapes from before Christianity. Marrying medieval literature with archeological discoveries, and applying anthropological principles to these analyses, yields glimpses at a fairly comprehensive heathen theological system.

Germanic northern Europe was polytheistic; that is, its religion included multiple gods. These gods are household names due to popular films as well as the days of the week—early English Tiw's Day became Tuesday, Thursday from Thor's Day, and so on. While these gods mostly came from the same family—Thor was Odin's son, for instance—polytheism can accommodate different cultures, and medieval literature tells of people who worshipped Christ alongside other Norse deities. Heathenism also involved veneration of ancestors and the dead, as well as landscapes and spirits of nature. It appears that reputation and honor were key motivations in heathen theology.

However, calling this a "religion" is imposing a standardized system onto an ill-defined and highly localized world view. Heathens did not set up a pantheon of "good" and "bad" gods, or compose holy books about what to believe, or insist that there was a single "truth" about the world that only some people held. They performed their local customs in the belief that they were the right way to go about things. And the "right way" varied from valley to fjord, from one farmstead to another, and likely even between generations as families grew or moved around.

Not until institutionalized Christianity appeared, that is, an organized religion that required communal faith and worship, did heathens even start to think of their practices as a philosophy.

An interesting thing about heathenism is that, while tied into nature and the landscape, it travels well. Iceland was essentially unpopulated before Norse settlers arrived in the late ninth century and then functioned as a majority-heathen society for over a century, including the establishment of sacred areas in previously uninhabited land (see chapter 4). The famous Eiríkr "the Red" (*rauði*) was a heathen, to his Christian wife's chagrin, and the two lived separately in their preferred ways in Greenland. Centuries earlier, the Angles, Saxons and Jutes brought their heathen practices to Britain and instituted Germanic holy sites and placenames. Where heathens went, their practices followed. Therefore, it is not at all surprising that heathenism came to Dublin along with its Norse inhabitants.

THE LANDSCAPE OF DYFLIN

This is evident in the set-up of the Norse town, elements of which persisted through the early modern period or even to the present day. The precise layout and limits of the pre-Norman town are still under consideration, but we know it was in the general area of central Dublin, where the Wood Quay civic offices of Dublin City Council now stand.

The Long Stone or *Langstein*, a man-made standing stone or monolith, was twelve to fourteen feet high and stood until removed in the early eighteenth century. Its site is now commemorated with a much smaller sculpture. While this site is now several hundred meters from the quay, it would have been a fixed navigation aide for sailors in Dublin Bay in the ninth and tenth centuries, and likely marked the edge of navigable passage in the tidal Liffey.[2]

There is not necessarily a religious dimension to this practical guide; however, the amount of effort to erect such a monolith indicates an interest in broadcasting power. It may also have had other functions, such as a marker of the space between the town and the bay.

More likely to be a symbol of specifically Norse power, however, is the burial mound or mounds that occupied what was once called Hoggen Green. It is now called College Green thanks to its nextdoor neighbor of Trinity College, the University of Dublin. There was a convent in the area founded in 1146 called St. Mary de Hogges, and sometimes historians presume that the green was named after the convent. However, Hoggen Green was named for its original function as a visible burial ground, "Hoggen" coming from Old Norse *haugr* (nominative + definite article *hauginn*, the mound).[3]

Dramatic interment of the dead is a universal human phenomenon, from ancient monuments like Newgrange and the Pyramids of Giza to modern mausolea like that of Elvis in Graceland. In addition to statements about the afterlife, prominent tombs announce prestige in the effort expended to create them, and they indicate a claim on the land by virtue of kinship—real or fictitious—with the deceased. The mound at the Hoggen, possibly the singular "hauginn," which made it all the way to the late seventeenth century before being demolished, is shown on the map in orange. Consider that this would have been highly visible to incoming sailors, particularly as they navigated the tidal River Liffey by utilizing the Langstein, and think as to how the Norse manipulation of the landscape signaled their conquest and occupation. Then imagine that there may have been a whole field of these impressive mounds on display!

The Hogges may have been the site of a ship burial like that of the Oseberg or Gokstad sites in Norway, where a wealthy individual or family was interred on a ship laden with goods for the afterlife, and a mound raised around the remains. The treatment of human remains is a good indicator of religious practice in medieval northern Europe. Inhumations or burials without grave goods, especially in churchyards buried with their heads to the west and feet to the east, are generally Christian. Meanwhile the presence of grave goods, and cremation, are signs of a non-Christian burial; but this is how the people who buried the body chose to depose their dead, not necessarily what the living person believed.

Unfortunately with its demolishment, the Hogges and anything else in the area is unavailable for archeological investigation of the medieval period. In fact, it is possible that the fill from the mound was utilized in the elevation of nearby Nassau Street, which occurred soon afterwards in an anti-flood effort. To this day, the busy street along Trinity College's southern border is approximately ten feet (three meters) higher than the campus. Perhaps students and city residents lining up in queues for Dublin buses do so with fragments of grave goods and inhumations crumbled to dust beneath their feet.

There lies a site of definite heathen interest between Hoggen Green and the Norse town proper: this space between where people lived in the west and died in the east. This area was known as the *Thingmotte* in later medieval Dublin, the first half of which comes from the Norse term for a proto-parliament "*thing*." This survives in other countries of Norse settlement in name, such as Iceland's Þingvellir, Norway's Gulatinget, Tingwall in the Orkneys, and Tynwald Hill in the Isle of Man. These are the areas that were specially used for administration and legal cases.

In the absence of a state or overarching structure such as the

Roman Church, self-imposed law assumed a religious component. Criminals did not just harm their victims and victims' families, but society as a whole, and made restitution by returning to the prior and "proper" ways of existence. Therefore the thing was held sacred throughout the Norse world as a site where gods and ancestors could receive proper deference by the establishment and resumption of an orderly society. The power of the thing continued after Christianization but in a secular fashion, and even today several Nordic countries and territories use thing-related words for their parliamentary bodies.

For centuries, confusion over the "motte" ending, which looks like "mount," led historians and amateurs alike to assume that the Hogges mound was the Thingmotte. But in a 2005 article Seán Duffy deftly identifies that the Thingmotte was a distinct region "just outside the city's eastern gate, straddling [modern] Dame Street, and lying to the west of Hoggen Green."[4] Duffy explains that "motte" is actually from the archaic English word "moot," related to our modern English word "meeting." The Thingmotte was still in use as a site of judicial administration by the time Henry II visited Dublin, which he used for his own law court in the winter of 1171–72. Its position just outside the town, but not within it, and linking the town to its burial ground, indicates the power and prestige of the thing in Norse Dublin.

Another site of specific importance for heathenism in Dublin is a site mentioned in literary sources, but whose location is not well-defined. This is *Caill Tomair* or the Wood of Thor, which I have with some temerity reconstructed into Old Norse as **Þorsviðr* (the preceding asterisk indicates that the word does not actually exist in contemporary documents). *Tomar* follows several established mechanisms for rendering Norse into Irish language: *Þ* becomes *T*,[5] and the medial *m* is softened in the grammatical form called lenition or *séimhiú*, which helps recreate the long *ó* ending in the rhotic *rr* into a similar vocal movement in Middle Irish. The existence of this translation suggests how important the god Thor was to the Norse who interacted with the Gaels. Within poetry, the Norse in Ireland are referred to as *muintir Tomair*, the tribe or family of Thor.[6]

Caill Tomair appears several times in the Irish annals and the *Cogadh Gáedhel re Gallaibh*, which is a Munster text written in the first quarter of the twelfth century that purports to give the history of the Norse in Ireland. Brian Boru is the star of this text, as it was composed for a descendant, most likely his great-grandson, Muircheartach Ua Briain. The overarching theme of the *Cogadh* is the prestige that Brian, and therefore his descendants, deserve for his subjugation of Norse and Gael alike. As a result, whether the historical Brian actually did so or not, the author of the text depicts him destroying sacred sites and royal symbols of his rivals all over Ireland. Therefore, when Brian's forces capture Dublin in 1000, they make firewood out of Caill Tomair as part of the city's subjugation.

This was apparently such a massive undertaking that fourteen years later, when an attendant describes the Battle of Clontarf to the elderly Brian, he compares the noise and confusion to the sound and sight of chopping down Caill Tomair and setting it ablaze. Because of this, and the fact that presumably fourteen years wasn't enough time for the grove to recover, it is unlikely that Caill Tomair was the same wood northeast of Dublin that trapped many of the Norse fleeing from Clontarf in the rising tide. In his 2014 book on Brian and the battle, Duffy suggests that Caill Tomair was near Dublin although well outside of the town, and may have been in the area of modern Phoenix Park.[7]

ARTIFACTS

Sites like burial mounds and sacred groves are powerful signs of ownership that can be used and re-used by subsequent leaders of an area. While not as immediately visible to all, portable objects can also be used as symbols of power. The Uí Néill king Mael Sechnaill II subjugated Dublin in 995, just a few years before Brian Boru. This subjugation included the possession of two artifacts from the Norse, described as the Sword of Carlus (*cloidhemh Carlusa*) and the Ring of Thor (*fail Tomair*).

Who "Carlus" was is not known for sure, but it is likely a version of Frankish name *Carolus*. Duffy remarks in his 2014 book that this name appears among the Dublin Norse in the form of a Carlus mac Amlaíb (whose name would be "Karl" or *Karlus? Óláfsson in Norse) whose death is recorded in the Irish annals in 868.[8] Therefore the Sword of Carlus may have been his literal sword, or ascribed to him, or perhaps he and the sword had the same namesake. In any event, the sword of Carlus, whose name was recorded over a century after Carlus mac Amlaíb's death, was likely kept for ancestral veneration and/or a sign of military authority, lending it authority as a symbol of Dublin.

The second artifact is described as Fail Tomair, the same "Tomar" that we saw is the Irish rendition of the Norse god Þórr or Thor. "Fail" in Middle Irish can refer to a number of circular or round objects, and it is usually translated in this case as an arm ring; it could potentially also refer to an enclosure, but it sounds like an object that was taken into Mael Sechnaill's possession. The Fail Tomair was almost certainly part of a heathen tradition of sacred rings used in the swearing of oaths that were specifically associated with the god Thor.

Both the ancestral sword of Carlus and the godly arm ring of Thor were likely used in oath ceremonies, particularly of a liegeman to his lord. This is a prominent plot point in Germanic medieval literature from Icelandic sagas to *Beowulf* to Old High German romances. Mael Sechnaill receiving the Sword of Carlus and the Ring of Thor was a symbol of his takeover of the town, a transfer of ruling power from the king of Dublin to his new over-king.

Unfortunately the sword and ring are no longer extant, or at least not yet recovered in archaeology or identified. There are, however, items of interest housed in the National Museum of Ireland that hint at heathenism in Dublin on an individual level. While not currently on display, there is a fragment of an iron staff recovered from Kilmainham, a section of central modern Dublin south of the River Liffey which was west of the Norse town of Dyflin and has revealed a rich source of inhumations. The iron staff is dated on account of its contemporary artifacts to the ninth century.

Neil Price includes it among several dozen artifacts found across the Norse world that he believes to be staves (plural of staff) that were utilized in heathen magical practices.[9] These ornamented iron objects, frequently buried in graves with wealthy goods associated with women, have been miscategorized as cooking spits and whip shanks, but Price argues that they are too decorated to be practical implements. Furthermore, these staves fit with the descriptions in medieval literature of a Norse witch or seer, one description of which is found in the aforementioned *Cogadh* (this incident is covered in chapter 2).

As previously mentioned, heathenism did not conceive of itself as a religion until it encountered opposition. Heathenism became self-aware with the presence of Christian missionaries in Scandinavia, including Iceland. Archaeology shows the manufacture of pendants

Fig. 1.1. Casting mold from Trendgården, Jutland.
Courtesy of National Museum of Denmark

shaped like *Mjölnir* or Thor's hammer to be worn as a symbol of heathenism, as opposed to the Christian cross or crucifix that Christians and missionaries would wear. Consider this soapstone mold from Denmark, which allowed the silversmith to generate a cross or a hammer depending on what their client wanted:

While heathenism is polytheist and thus involves many gods, Thor is described in Norse literature as a particular friend and protector of the people. One of the holy symbols of Thor, Mjölnir—the hammer he utilizes to keep brutish giants away from humans—serves as a synecdoche, or part to represent the whole, of heathenism. Heathens who wanted to complement the cross of Christians chose a stylized Mjölnir to wear. As we have seen, Thor's name is associated with both a wood and a sacred object for the Norse at Dublin. He may have been the focal god for the families that settled in Ireland, whether from their ancestral homeland or as members of the Irish Norse-Gaelic community.

The use of pendants to mark one's religion is not a certainty as to someone's beliefs, but then again, nothing in archaeology really is. Nonetheless, it at least indicates that someone wants to depict themselves as such. Therefore, the existence of a Mjölnir pendant, whether buried with a body intentionally or dropped into the floor of a house accidentally, indicates that someone wanted to show themselves as a heathen. While the National Museum of Ireland does not officially have any Mjölnir pendants in its collection, it houses several objects that could be reconsidered as potential hammers or symbols of heathenism. Several amber pendants previously classified as crosses, or unidentified, will be explored by me in a forthcoming chapter of *More Tales from Medieval Dublin* from Four Courts Press.

In a 2015 book chapter entitled "Meagre Lead," Patrick F. Wallace, the former director of the National Museum, reclassifies a number of items that had previously been categorized as lead fishing line weights.* Instead of pragmatic items, Wallace now describes these lead alloy objects as cross pendants and "anchors," specifically ". . . functionless ornaments—a kind of 3D doodle."[10] I find it difficult to accept that the production of cross pendants alongside these hammer-looking objects is purely coincidental. If an artisan is creating cross pendants out of lead in Norse Dublin, why cannot we

*As of 2022, they are still labeled as such in the museum.

consider that they are also creating lead Mjölnir-shaped pendants as well?

CONVERSION IN DYFLIN

While Norse Dublin was considered to have been well aware of Christianity for centuries from their Gaelic Irish neighbors as well as in continental trade, nonetheless it contained heathen elements in its landscape, and its residents would not have necessarily considered themselves entirely Christian before the eleventh century. And even then, all we have is archeology—landscape and objects—to suggest what those who had authority wished to display.

The oldest church in Dyflin is Christchurch Cathedral, originally founded by King Sitric *Silkiskeggi*, or Silkenbeard, after his pilgrimage to Rome in 1028. Christchurch looked to Canterbury in England rather than to local Irish church authority, so while there were Gaelic churches in the area previously, this served as *Norse* Dublin's first church of its own. Sitric was the first man in Ireland to mint his own coins, on an Anglo-Saxon model, and his sponsorship of Christchurch is in line with his desire to emulate English and continental Christian kingship.[11] But this is a display of power and authority, not necessarily a sweeping stamp of the religious practices and faiths of all residents of Dyflin at the time.

The spread of Christianity is often treated as an inevitable and irreversible process, and most scholars of this period simply assume that the Irish were irrevocably Christian, thus the eventual conversion of the Norse was aided by the established religion of their fellow countrymen (and wives). Christchurch looked far away to Canterbury, rather than to Armagh in the north, a sign of the political benefits of conversion into an international system of privilege rather than a hearty acceptance of local Christianity. If the Norse in Ireland were sold on Christianity by their baptized household members and neighbors, why didn't they buy into the Irish Church?

Private personal practice, as well, would have continued long after church bells rang out over Dyflin. Just as the conversion to Christianity in Iceland was a social one, where practices in individual households were not initially legislated (see chapter 4), townspeople in Dyflin likely would have persisted in their habits and customs indoors, even if heathen in origin or anti-Christian in practice. Vernacular expressions of power and status, the balance of gender roles and expectations within a working household, and the cycles of annual holidays and ceremonies to mark life achievements rarely change overnight. In particular, a domestic situation with enslaved people in close proximity can struggle with the Christian religion that purports the fundamental equality of all practitioners, regardless of identity.

This is not to say that heathen rites were carried out as spiteful acts of defiance or subversion, but rather that a conversion of the body is not necessarily a conversion of the spirit. Who knows what people believe and perform behind closed doors? Modern Dublin uses 841CE as its founding date, though the actual size and continuation of the town through the turbulent ninth century is not fully understood.[12] If we use this date, then Dyflin functioned for 187 years without its own church; at least nine generations of Norse speakers occupying the mouth of the Liffey without Christian authority.

With the presence of sites like Caill Tomhair and the burial mounds, Dyflin was a large-scale demonstration of the ability of Norse beliefs to be carried out of Scandinavia and planted to flourish in new soils abroad. The erection of monuments like the Langstein were intentional claims on the landscape, but every stone and post planted on the banks of the Liffey and Poddle and Dodder were also testaments to heathen ingenuity and perseverance in settling new land overseas. The possible Thor's hammers (**uird Tomhair*) in amber and lead could also demonstrate the willingness of the residents of Dyflin to create and demonstrate their faith in a symbol.

DYFLIN IN THE NORTH ATLANTIC

In our modern world of land-based transit and national boundaries, it is sometimes difficult to conceive of a sea-based political entity whose centers of power are marine rather than terrestrial. This is covered in more detail in chapter 3 on the island kingdom(s). For the Vikings and their descendants, Dyflin was a bright star in the constellation of Norse-speaking ports and trading centers across the North Atlantic. By the year 1000, Norse was spoken from what is now North America at L'anse aux Meadows and the Greenlandic settlements, across Europe and into the Mediterranean, in modern Kiev, in modern Istanbul by members of the Varangian Guard (who called their city of Constantinople *Miklagarðr* or "Mighty Fortress"), and likely further east and south in the form of trading outposts and mercenaries. Dyflin was central in this vast network.

Unfortunately, the Norse also participated heavily in the international slave trade. They trafficked native Gaels, and other foreigners, through the Dyflin slave market. This may have resulted in Gaels living in the manner of their Norse captors. While coercion and consent are obviously a concern in this situation, medieval slavery was seen as an imposition on a person rather than an inherent quality of the enslaved. For example, in the Icelandic *Laxdæla Saga* of circa 1245, while distributing her estate, Unnr says, ". . . I have made a free man of Erp, the son of Earl Meldoon [Maeldúin, a Gaelic name]. It was far from my intention that such a well-born man be called a slave."[11] Many slaves would be freed, and then with that freedom, they could choose to continue in the manner they had spent much of their lives, especially if they had been trafficked as children. This would be another way people of Gaelic origin came to live in Hiberno-Norse towns, the exemplar of which was Dyflin.

Eventually, the intermarriage of Gaelic and Norse families resulted in the political Christianization of the Hiberno-Norse, at the same time that Norse kings of Scandinavia were converting elsewhere in northern Europe. But before this, there were generations of Norse who came to Ireland and practiced their pre-Christian religious traditions. It is sometimes difficult to imagine picking up and relocating a land-based spirituality, but heathenry is adaptable. Just as Frisians, Angles, Jutes, and Saxons bring their gods to and make holy spaces in what is now Great Britain, Ireland was no different, and Dyflin was the city *par excellence* of this process.

2
Elsewhere in Ireland
Norse-Gaelic Towns and Landscapes

While Dyflin was the largest town in medieval Ireland and a significant port in the trading network of Norse speakers across northern Europe and the Atlantic, it was not the only Norse-Gaelic settlement on the island of Ireland. As at Dyflin, Vikings were able to gain footholds in Ireland at riverine communities that were not already well-established and far from the nearest centers of local power. Consequentially, these settlements, when successful, became themselves important political sites, coveted by local Gaelic kings due to the international presence and taxable wealth of Norse trade and technology.

The survival of the "Viking towns" to the present in modern Ireland is a curious facet of Irish history. Four of the best-known—Dublin, Limerick, Waterford, and to a lesser extent but increasingly Cork—are also among the leading cities of the Republic of Ireland. Wexford, the fifth, is now "merely" a county town, but has served as an interesting outpost of foreign settlement throughout the medieval and early modern periods due to its geographical proximity to Britain and mainland Europe.*

The history of these towns demonstrates what is known as "survival bias," where their importance in the Norse incursions to Ireland is assumed and perhaps inflated because they are still relevant political entities today. Conversely, this complicates their archeology, because the fleeting traces of temporary settlement and early foundations are much more likely to have disappeared under later development in an area with centuries of continual occupation.

The earliest settlement of what is now Waterford has likely been discovered, with a healthy dose of skepticism, at a far less-populated area upriver, now called Woodstown. But the first "ship-camp" (*longphort*) of what is now Dublin has never been definitively found, and is unlikely to be recovered in the silt and continuous rebuilding of the capitol city and its environs (see chapter 1).

There were also Viking outposts that were not successful, and thus are rarely mentioned outside of historical studies. Their failure and isolation, however, can result in a richly preserved archeological record. The exemplar is the longphort called *Linn Duachaill*, Duachall's Pool, mentioned in *Cogadh Gáedhel re Gallaibh* and several Irish annals, which was discovered and identified between 2005 and 2010; more on Linn Duachaill below.

There are also sites that are only known by written history, such as a settlement on Strangford Lough in Northern Ireland, mentioned in the *Chronica Regum Manniæ et Insularum* (*Chronicle of the Kings of Man and the Isles*). This Norse presence is preserved

*To this day, and even more so post-Brexit, the primary port between Ireland and the rest of the European Union is found in Rosslare Harbour, County Wexford.

in the English language name itself: Strangford from *Strongfjörðr*, "strong ford," referring to the immense tides.[1] The powerful local presence of the Uí Néill dynasty and its offshoots discouraged longterm Norse occupation in Strangford and other areas in the north of Ireland.*

Without a written record, isolated archeological discoveries may also offer tantalizing glimpses at: Norse settlement(s) in Ireland outside of towns, the ready incorporation of items of Norse manufacture into Gaelic households, very early Norse-Gaelic blending that brought families out of towns into farmsteads or landholdings, or phenomena beyond these ideas.

LINN DUACHAILL

Linn Duachaill was found near a small village named Annagassan (*Áth na gCasán*) in County Louth and dates to the same founding year as Dyflin. But because Linn Duachaill failed to succeed as a town, the settlement was abandoned, and its remains are well-preserved beneath lightly disturbed farmland. The modern village of Annagassan seized upon the Norse connection nearly as soon as the artifacts came to light, and the village hosted several years of a "Viking Festival."

Ten miles north of Annagassan is the town of Dundalk (*Dún Dealgan*), on a deeper and less tidal harbor. Here, according to the *Cathréim Cellacháin Cháisil*, was the site of an intense naval battle in the tenth century between Gaelic and Norse forces, led by Cellachán mac Buadacháin and Sitriuc mac Tuirgeis respectively. Geoffrey Keating put this battle into his seventeenth century *History*

*Ironically, it can be argued that a *lack* of Norse towns in Uí Néill territory was to their economic disadvantage, in the long run, by not having established urban centers.

of Ireland (*Foras Feasa ar Éirinn*), with a flair for the dramatic that has made subsequent historians dismiss the whole event as a legend. But it is possible that the memory of the Norse in Ireland, in the mind of *Cellacháin*'s author, included a battle on or near the sea at Linn Duachaill.

LIMERICK

Luimneach in Middle Irish, Limerick is transposed into Old Norse as *Hlymrekr*. *Cogadh* describes a fort and a "good town" (*degbali*)[2] there. It is unclear if there are also residences within the fort, as Brian's men enter the fort and then slaughter the Norse "on the streets and in the houses" (*ar na srathaib ⁊ isna taigib*).[3] The Norse who escape regroup in the "western harbour of Limerick" (*iartharach Lumnig*),[4] the seaward side of the River Shannon.

A similar scene in *Cellacháin* sees the titular character's forces go into Limerick, where the Norse cannot "close the gates" (*na doirsi na dunad*) of the fort and are slaughtered "in the houses and in the towers" (*isna tignibh ⁊ isna toraibh*). There are civilians present in Limerick, as the Norse give up "their wives and children [*lit.* dear sons] and households" (*mna ⁊ a maccaemha ⁊ a muintera*) to Cellachán and his men.[5]

WATERFORD

Waterford is Port Láirge, Lárag's Port, in Middle Irish and Veðrafjörður ("Wether [i.e., Ram] Fjord") in Old Norse. In the saga of Cerball, the Norse are driven "into a small town with stone fortification around it" (*i mbaile beg ⁊ cloch dhaingean ime*) and one of their leaders goes "up onto the rampart" (*ar an chaisiol*).[6] The

Norse are besieged and a few of them escape, with wealthy spoils and "beautiful women left behind" (*ban caomh ro fagbhaid ann sin*),[7] indicating the presence of noncombatants.

Waterford also hosts civilians in *Cellacháin* and may have been the designated place for the families of Norse across Munster. Cellachán's men capture Limerick, Cork, and Cashel within the narrative and then go to Waterford. After winning a battle outside the town, they go "where the women and families of the Norse were" (*a rabhatar mna ⁊ muinntera na Lochlannach*) then burn the "town" (*baili*). Cellachán's forces then go onto the "green" (*faigthi*) of Waterford, when a fleet of Norse ships arrives. The Norse already in Waterford close "the gates" (*doirsi*) and attempt to defend themselves; nonetheless they are defeated once more by Cellachán and his men.[8]

CORK

The Norse name for Cork is unknown. *Corcaigh* means "marshy land," likely referring to the city's establishment on the islands of the River Lee, where it spreads into a delta on its way to Lough Mahon and the protection of Cobh Harbour. Perhaps it had a name that was a Norse version of this appellation, such as **Saurseyjar*, Marsh-Islands. It is tempting to draw a parallel with modern York, *Jórvík* in Norse, and come up with something like **Kornvík*, Grain Bay, but York's name is ancient—*Eborakon*, as recorded by Ptolemy in 150 CE—and the Norse was merely the contemporary version of the name. But it is more likely that Cork had a name used by its Norse inhabitants and contemporaries that has now fallen out of historical reach.

Until recently, the main evidence for Cork's Viking presence was the place-name Keyser's Lane, for a narrow footpath running steeply down to the river, a feature also found near the early medieval harbors of Dublin, Waterford, and Wexford. It was deduced as early as the sixteenth century that this similarly-named feature across these towns must be of Norse origin, and assumed by context to mean something like "the steep path to the water."[9]

But the actual relationship of "Keyser" to the Norse language is unclear, particularly as *key* for *quay*, the modern term for mercantile city wharves, derives from French.

Fortunately, however, the 2009 closure of the Beamish brewery* across the Lee from Keyser's Hill made the land available for archeological excavation. Many discoveries have been made and more are surely forthcoming about Viking-era Cork.

Norse towns in these three Middle Irish texts are described with nearby greens (*faichi*, plural form of *faithche* and variants), a town (baile, singular form of *baili*), and a fort (dún) or other enclosure that can be closed with a gate (*doirse*, singular form of *doirsi*). In Dublin, the fort seems to have been separate from the living quarters of the town, although both Amlaibh† and Sitriuc have a personal connection to the fort. Noncombatants reside within the gates in Limerick and Waterford. Little is said about the harbors, which must have been vital for these towns, nor the mechanisms by which they collected tribute and supplies from their hinterlands. These ninth- and tenth-century Viking towns of the Irish imagination give us a snapshot of the eleventh- and twelfth-century Hiberno-Norse reality they encountered, which is hidden from us today by centuries of development.

---

*Unfortunately for stout drinkers.

†According to the vagaries of Middle Irish orthography, Amlaíb and Amlaibh may be the same person under two slightly different spellings.

ECCLESIASTICAL CENTERS: CASHEL, ARMAGH, KILDARE, CLONMACNOISE

While early medieval Ireland did not have Roman-style urbanity, falling outside the remit of the Roman Empire in archeology if not philosophy, there were nonetheless proto-towns. These were the ecclesiastical centers, established around important churches and monastic communities, and surely housing as many or more secular "laity" (that is, people who are *not* priests, monks, nuns, etc.) as people involved in the Christian Church. These centers would absorb pilgrims, merchants, and other visitors at special times throughout the year such as saints' days and market fairs, but they also hosted a sustained population throughout the year that required regular importation of food and other goods from the countryside around it.

Famously, or stereotypically, the Vikings preferred to attack monastic settlements across northern Europe, as they were both full of portable wealth and populated with noncombatants. However, these monasteries were often the nucleus of trade networks and complicated political entanglements with powerful dynasties, who filled the hierarchy of the local church with their less military-minded sons. This was particularly evident in Ireland, where the control of large churches was an important political bargaining chip for leading families. In this way, the Norse towns were both exotic imports of urban living, but also familiar to anyone who lived in or near an ecclesiastical center.

Armagh (*Ard Macha*) and Cashel (*Caisel*) were the archbishops' seats of the northern half of the island and the southern half, respectively.* As the home of these leading cathedrals, Armagh

*To this day, the Church of Ireland is divided in half between the Province of Armagh and the United Provinces of Cashel and Dublin.

and Cashel attracted clerics and lay people alike to collect, display, and distribute prestige items—as well as to merely feed, clothe, and service the church officials there. Before the twelfth-century synods that restructured the administration of the Church in Ireland, powerful monasteries dedicated to important saints had similar powers, especially if well-situated to benefit from multiple dynasts' provisions, or geography conducive to trade. Kildare (*Cill Dara*), the cathedral founded by Saint Brigid, "the Mary of the Gaels," was a prime example of this.

Therefore, when Vikings came to Ireland in search of easy wealth, noncombatants to traffick into slavery, and already-established seats of power, the ecclesiastical centers were an obvious choice. *Cellachain* suggests that Cashel and Armagh became Norse strongholds in the ninth century, despite their locations far inland. Armagh in particular seemed to have merely changed hands without an expulsion or mass slaughter of the population; when the main character comes to the gate of Armagh, it is "guarded" by a fellow Gael: the bishop himself![9] It would be impractical, even foolish, for the Norse in Ireland to establish themselves somewhere far from the sea and their characteristic ships. This was not only for reasons of military maneuverability, but because they were traders and travelers who kept their toehold in Ireland on account of their ability to flee, or call in reinforcements, by sea.

Another important ecclesiastical site was Clonmacnoise (*Cluan Mhic Nóis*), just upriver from Athlone (*Baile Átha Luain*, Town of Luan's Ford). On the enormous River Shannon, near the ford (*áth*) that permitted east-west passage across the otherwise impassable boundary, Clonmacnoise is located near the literal geographic center of Ireland yet also benefits from riverine traffic. *Cogadh* places the leader of the Norse in Ireland, Turges, at Clonmacnoise, where he sets himself to receive the tribute normally given to the church.

Irish "Turges" has been put into Norse several ways: *Þórkels*, *Þurgestr*, *Þórgísl*, and so on. According to the *Annals of Ulster*, and *Cogadh*, the name is sometimes spelled "Tuirgeis" (among further variations). In narratives by Gerald of Wales (*Giraldus Cambrensis*), his name has been Latinized to *Turgesius*. Perhaps due to the lasting popularity of Gerald's works, the Viking leader's name is most often rendered in this Latinate form.

No definitive proof of his identity has been found outside of Irish and British documents, although some scholars have argued in a roundabout way that contextually he is Ragnar Loðbrok of Icelandic heroic saga fame.[10] It is also possible he is the unnamed "king of the Vikings" met by Muslim envoy al-Ghazal, found in the story "An amusing book from poetical works of the *Maghrib* [West]" (*Al-mutrib min ashar ahli'l Maghrib*) by Abu-l-Kattab-Umar-ibn-al-Hasan-ibn-Dihya.[11]

Because Turges only exists in Irish sources, it is possible this name is not Norse in origin. I propose a novel interpretation of his name, beginning with the second element "ge(i)s." This word descends from Old Irish *guidid*, to pray—a native term, not a Latin import such as many Christian terms of worship are in Ireland, indicating a pre-Christian concept. *Geis*, plural *gessi*, appears in early Irish literature as prohibitions or requirements of people, imposed by supernatural figures or divination that must be followed to avoid disaster.[12] "Turge(i)s" thus would imply a person bound by some kind of holy imposition.

The first element may be *tur*, dryness, making his name something like "prohibition to be dry"—a fitting title for a man who met an ignominious end, being drowned in a lake! Another possibility, seeing as Tomhar is Irish for Old Icelandic Þórr (see chapter 1), is that "Tur" designates a Norse god, perhaps Old Icelandic Týr, who is otherwise unattested in Irish sources. This would make Turges mean "charged by/sacred to Týr," or maybe "Þórr." As the non-Christianity of the Norse in Ireland was particularly scandalous for the clerical authors of these histories, it is possible that the name for this "king of the Vikings" is an Irish appellation that preserves, or mocks, his supernatural dealings.

WHAT WAS LIFE LIKE IN AN IRISH NORSE TOWN?

While the streets and shape of Dyflin are fairly well known, much of the archeology and shape of the other Norse towns in Ireland can only be guessed. The appearance of those towns' hinterlands, and isolated farmsteads beyond, is even less known. They are ghosts of conjecture today. But for the people who lived in, traveled through, worked in, traded with, or were enslaved in these Norse-Gaelic interfaces, they were solid, smelly, imposing, and very real. And like towns and cities today, they would have been updated; expanded; subject to fires, floods, and other natural disasters; rebuilt; with portions no longer needed left vacant and gone to ruin. Even if we could peer into a telescope and see what Limerick was like in the year 900, it would bear little resemblance to Limerick in 1000.

But also like towns and cities today, these meeting points and nexuses of trade would produce a rapid and vibrant culture fostered by so many people living and moving through the same small area. There must have been some pidgin or creole language* allowing Old Norse and Middle Irish speakers to communicate, especially

*The survival of such a language is considered in chapter 3.

because the usual cross-cultural language, Latin, had not yet penetrated Scandinavia in the form of an extensive clerical network. There was regular intermarriage, particularly between Norse men and Gaelic women. The sources tell of these couplings both between leading families for political gain and from enslaved people taken as concubines; there must have also existed the intermediate step of relatively free households with young adults choosing to marry each other despite the cultural divide.

Both Norse and Gaelic culture sent brides to the family of their husbands, though their loyalties and legal standings would still be somewhat entwined with their birth relatives. Married women were tasked with childcare in both cultures, meaning that the children of these Norse-Gaelic marriages were mostly raised under the care of their mothers' cultural values. The wealthiest women would have nurses and household helpers to assist, however, and the husband's sisters and other female relatives would surely have contributed, particularly if the mother died or became incapacitated. But there was still a considerable amount of matrilineal influence, even in cases of enslavement or other drastic differences in social standing between mother and father.

This indicates that, even in "Norse" households where that was the primary language, the presence of Irish-speaking mothers and servants or slaves would have given children in Irish Norse towns a foot in either culture as they grew. Furthermore, the system of fosterage, where children as young as seven were moved from their household out to extended family or trusted associates to raise and train, was found in both Irish and Norse contexts. This would have contributed to a seamless integration of the two separate linguistic communities for the generations raised in them. Consider as well that those children grew to be the next residents and craftspeople in the towns, and the leaders of nearby Gaelic dynasties who saw the financial and social advantages of integrating with the Norse in Ireland. It would only take two or three generations, even with regular interchange and immigration with the rest of the Norse-speaking world, for the townspeople in Ireland to be comfortable inhabitants of a Norse-Gaelic interface, a community whole and of itself. The towns depended on agriculture and goods from their hinterlands to survive, as well as overseas commerce, but they were not precarious marginalized areas at a disadvantage from being neither wholly Gaelic nor Norse.

The question then is, what does this mean for Norse-Gaelic paganism? Gaelic residents of Norse towns in Ireland, whether there by choice nor coercion, certainly witnessed Norse heathen practices they encountered within their domiciles and/or the larger community. It must be considered possible that they may have participated in them. For instance, consider the appearance of a ritual practiced in Clonmacnoise, described in the *Cogadh*:

> *. . . is and do-bered Ota ben Turges a (h-uricli)/(frecartha) ar altoir Cluana mic Nois.*
>
> . . . the place where Ota, the wife of Turges, gave her [audience]/[answers] was upon the altar of Clonmacnoise [Cathedral].[13]

Uricli, "audience," is the word used in one of three extant copies of the *Cogadh*, whereas *frecartha*, "answers," is found in both the oldest and least complete, and the youngest and most complete, copies. Either way, both are usually understood in scholarship to refer to magical practices that appear in Norse sources as *spae* or *seiðr*.

In these episodes, a (typically) female seer occupies an elevated position where she answers questions or makes pronouncements for her audience, based on her ability to perceive a spirit-world or afterlife from her seat. The most famous example of this in Norse literature occurs in *Eirikr Saga Rauðr*, though it is mentioned in other sagas and semi-historical narratives. These include the Arabic narrative from Ahmad ibn Fadlān al-'Abbas ibn Rāshid ibn Hammād, which reports an enslaved woman being lifted up to see and describe "Paradise" before her death.[14] The appearance of a Norse ritual with this shared elevation-and-sight function across such disparate medieval textual sources as an Icelandic saga and an account by an envoy from Bagdad indicates that there was *something* to this, even if only in reference to imagined heathen practices by non-heathen authors.

Adding the half-sentence from *Cogadh* to this corpus strengthens the argument, but, it is a weak bit of evidence on its own. To begin with, the historical existence of Turges himself is unknown, whether or not he was known by that name outside of Ireland. Presuming he did live at one time and had a wife, what precisely was *she* doing "upon the altar" (*ar altoir*) at Clonmacnoise? The passage is among a litany of outrages Turges and his people wreak upon Ireland, particularly upon its churches, although the complaints are more often related to the collection of tithes and displacement of church officials. Named women are hard to find in Irish dynastic narratives, particularly Norse women, so at the very least there is something concerning enough about Ota's action to record it for posterity. Perhaps it is the very profanity of a woman *ar altoir* that offends the author of the *Cogadh*.

If so, why try to explain what she was doing there? The survival of two different versions of this passage, enticingly in chronologically disparate manuscripts, suggests that the explanation was worth recording as well as amending later. The multipurpose verb *do-beir* can indicate giving, understanding, bringing, or other meanings of conveyance. The relationship of Ota to either her audience or to her answers is, frankly, unknown.

It is convenient to assume that both versions are true and Ota was *ar altoir* to provide "answers" to the questions of her "audience" and thus neatly fold this into evidence of seiðr or other magic performed by a woman. But it is a tautological problem, not dissimilar to the titular one posed by Frank in "The Boar on the Helmet," where the chance revenants of the medieval past become irrevocably linked to one another by dint of their shared survival.[15]

Readers taking an interest in the original language may have noticed that "gall" is translated as "foreigner," while the word in Irish that refers to the Norse, thus far, is *Lochlannach*. Starting with J. H. Todd, the editor-translator of the *Cogadh*, there is over 150 years of scholarship on the Norse in Ireland that consider the specific words for them as diagnostic in some manner.* The overlap between annalistic terminology and the three documents in this chapter's purview is extensive, but not perfectly similar.

DANAIR AND LOCHLANNAIGH

The most common names for the Norse in pre-Norman Irish material are variations on *gaill* and "geinti," typically translated as "foreigner" and "heathen," and literally meaning "Gaul" (i.e., foreigner from overseas) and "gentile" (i.e., a non-Christian), respectively. These are often given the modifiers of *finn* and *dub*, over which gallons of ink has been spilled. There appear to be two groups of Vikings operating in the Irish Sea region as they war with

*The most comprehensive recent essay is Colmán Etchingham's 2014 "Names for the Vikings in Irish Annals."

each other throughout the chronologies. "Finn" means "white" or "shining," and "dub" means "black" or "dark," which has prompted many theories about literal or figurative whiteness and darkness.* According to the annals, the finn Norse were in Ireland first, so the dub are the "second wave."

It is important to distinguish that gaill and geinti are exonyms, names for a group of people given from outside of themselves; whether *Finngaill* or *Dubgeinti*, these terms were designed in the Irish language for a Gaelic audience. *Nordman* and variations are also recorded in the *Annals of Ulster* and the *Cogadh*. "Nordman" is an example of an endonym, a name for a group of people that comes from within; as modern English speakers we can see right away that these are the "North-men," and the term derives from how the Norse saw themselves.

Exonyms are often marginalizing and intrinsically othering, though they can also be taken on and adopted. "Gael," for instance, began as an exonym from Wales, deriving from Welsh *gwyddel* meaning pirate or marauder.[16] Endonyms still demarcate a group, but utilizing their self-made designation indicates a certain measure of cultural interchange and linguistic awareness. The other two terms for the Norse in medieval Irish literature, Lochlannaigh and Danair, illustrate an exonym versus endonym, respectively.

In general, although not without dissent, prevailing scholarship has equated pre-Norman Lochlann with Norway and the Danair as coming from Denmark. This has resulted in pop histories of Ireland, indeed the whole Irish Sea region, describing Norse conflicts from the ninth to twelfth century as between "Norwegians" and "Danes." The author of a current popular history text book

*The best recent article about this is Clare Downham's contribution to *Medieval Dublin XI*: "Viking identities in Ireland: it's not all black and white."

writes, for instance, that the "Vikings who attacked Ireland were mainly Norwegians."[17] Seeing as a unified kingdom named Norway did not exist until decades after the founding of Dublin, clearly the attacks were by time-travelers!

The "finn" and "dub" modifiers are identified with the Lochlannaigh and Danair respectively, and old ideas such that everyone from Norway was blond while everyone from Denmark was dark-haired are also wildly outdated. However, as we will see, the finn/dub Lochlannaigh/Danair association breaks down in twelfth-century literature, if it was ever meant to be used in a 1:1 manner.

The Danair and Lochlannaigh are opposing forces in both the *Cerball* saga and *Cogadh*, and both narratives depict the Lochlannaigh as the first wave or entrenched population within Ireland. The Lochlannaigh are an unwanted menace in *Cerball* while the Danair are the "helpful" Norse worthy of alliance for the Gaels, namely Cerball mac Dúnlainge.* This is reverse to the overall scenario within the *Cogadh*, where the Lochlannaigh are seen as a foreign albeit communicative people, and the Danair are the suddenly threatening interlopers in Ireland.[18] Does this have to do with Waterford and Wexford being Norse towns of a later founding date than the Lochlannaigh-settled Dublin, making the Danair the local and better-known group of Vikings in Osraige? The term Danair appears very infrequently within *Cellacháin*, as opposed to the overwhelming prevalence of Lochlannaigh within the text, that it is difficult to draw a comparison with the other two texts.

Each text, moreover, has terminology to describe the Norse as a culture or set of actions, especially *Cerball*, which features apostates

*This is the same Cerball of Osraige. The patronym mac *Dúnlainge* is his family ("son of Dungal"), and Osraige (Anglicized Ossory, in modern Counties Kilkenny and Laois) is the kingdom where he is from.

who are Gaelic Irish by birth but Norse by function: the Gall-Gaedil or Foreign Gaels introduced in the introduction. *Normannaigh* is the generic adjective in this text, while Gall is used for all Norse speakers in *Cogadh*, and "Lochlannaigh" performs this function in *Cellacháin*. Curiously, "Lochlannaigh" also has the umbrella role in the *Cathréim*, where it is used several times as a poetic synecdoche for all Norse from overseas; this quality skips over *Cogadh*, particularly the Brussels manuscript, where "Lochlannaigh" is only used a handful of times throughout the expansive narrative. However, the chapters that survive in the twefth-century *Book of Leinster*, approximately twenty percent of the completed story, proportionally use "Lochlannaigh" far more frequently. The seventeenth-century manuscript uses "geinti" and other words for pirates more often. This suggests a changing relationship in Irish conceptions of "Lochlannaigh."

What, then, is the relationship between Lochlann/d the place and Lochlannaigh the people? The potential ninth-century historical reality of an overseas kingdom aside, for the authors of these eleventh and twelfth-century narratives, the poorly defined *Lochlann/d* is a region outside of the Irish Sea region associated with the Norse of Ireland, who became associated with it on account of their shared language with it rather than literal origin there. Lochlann/d is faraway and foreign, specifically non-Irish,[19] and so with growing frequency for Middle Irish speakers, Norse speakers are all Lochlannaigh regardless of their place of residence or birth. While *Danmörg* or Denmark is also a territory overseas, it only appears in *Cogadh* in the form of the ethnonym *Danmargach*.

"Lochlannaigh" can be compared to any number of modern nicknames or slurs for a group of immigrants based on assuming they all come from one of several possible areas abroad. "Danair," on the other hand, is a loan-word from Old Norse to describe Norse speakers wherever they are; its use in the oldest text to distinguish the most pliant and Gael-adjacent group of Norse in Ireland suggests that the label in Irish came from regular and equitable relations with Norse speakers. The near-disappearance of "Danair" from *Cellacháin*, the youngest text, in favor of the potentially pejorative "Lochlannaigh" suggests that either the contemporary Norse speakers, the Hiberno-Norse, needed to be exoticised by the author, or that, by circa 1130, they had adopted and accepted the term for themselves. Perhaps, like the Gaels naming themselves after a Welsh exonym meaning "marauder," the pre-Norman Hiberno-Norse reclaimed and empowered themselves as an Irish people who once came from overseas.

3
The Northern and Southern Isles
Færeyjar to Mann

> The sea was first and foremost the glue that held these maritime kingdoms together; it was a highway that provided the main means of transportation and communication (what a Norse poet metaphorically referred to as "the sea king's way").[1]

A long chain of islands runs in a soft curve between the north of Ireland and mainland Britain, then northeast into the North Atlantic. Further to the northwest of the chain, the Faroe Islands lie towards Iceland, though it is still 350 nautical miles (660 km) or so of open ocean between them. With crenellated coastlines and hundreds of coves, natural harbors, and tide-dependent territories, these isles naturally served as the bases for the maritime dynasties and ship-borne warriors who came to Britain and Ireland from Scandinavia in the late eighth, ninth, and later centuries.

Centuries of naval warfare, international treaties, and cultural history have divided these isles into five subregions: the Isle of Man, the Hebrides (further split into Inner and Outer), the Orkneys, the Shetland Islands, and the Faroes. Man is an independent nation that functions internationally as a protectorate of the United Kingdom; the middle three island groups are fully a part of Scotland; and the Faroe Islands are an autonomous territory of the modern Kingdom of Denmark. It is easy in our land-based modern mindset to think of these three separate nations as distinct and isolated arms from a larger mainland. But to Vikings and their nautical descendants, the isles were an avenue of endless locales for setting up bases of attack, for opportune moorings and clandestine agreements, and for settling down into crofts and farmsteads in sight of the sea.

In the Norse conception of the North Atlantic world, these isles were grouped into three names: *Suðreyjar*, *Norðreyjar*, and Færeyjar. The Suðreyjar, or "Southern Isles," comprised the Isle of Man, the Inner and Outer Hebrides, the islands of the Clyde, and sometimes included portions of the coast of western Scotland. The difficulty traversing the Highlands meant that it was often easier to reach, and defend, the western coast of Scotland from the Hebrides than from the eastern Lowlands. The Norðreyjar, "Northern Isles," were the Orkneys (*Orkneyjar*) and Shetland (*Hjaltland*), and may have incorporated what is now Caithness (*Katanes*) and Sutherland (*Suðrland*, but left as "Sutherland" to not be confused with the Suðreyjar) in the extreme northeast of Scotland.

The Færeyjar are often translated as "Sheep (*fær*) Isles" after the domesticated animals found living wild on the islands by the Norse settlers who arrived there in the ninth century. But this is not known for certain. Their name may also be a Norse adoption of an early Irish word for the islands, as both archeological evidence and secondhand testimony from an eighth century Irish monk strongly suggest that Christian ascetics had set up sparse settlements there. At the very least, the presence of the sheep indicates prior human habitation, as they certainly didn't sail there themselves. Færeyjar could be from other words for travel (related to what became "far" and "faring" in modern English); this etymology would make a handy tripartite division between the isles as "South," "North," and "Further"!

Altogether, the islands appeared regularly in the histories and literature of the ninth through twelfth centuries, but produced no sustained documentation until soon after this period. The Suðreyjar feature in the mid-thirteenth century Latin-language *Chronicle of the Kings of Man and the Isles* (*Chronica Regum Manniæ et Insularum*), while the Norðreyjar are represented in the Old Icelandic *Orkneyinga Saga* of roughly the same date. The Færeyjar had their own thirteenth-century *Færeyinga Saga*, which is now missing, but portions of it appear in surviving Icelandic material. Unfortunately for Norse-Gaelic historians, this lack of contemporary literature leaves an enormous void in what was likely the most fertile and sustained interface of Norse and Gaelic culture in the North Atlantic.

THE NORSE-GAELIC HISTORY OF THE ISLES

The history of the isles in the ninth through twelfth centuries, then, is triangulated by three forms of evidence that are imperfect on their own but can be combined into more potent possibilities. The first is contemporary documentation from outside of the isles, mixed with later material that has happened to survive, such as the Icelandic settlement literature. The second is archeology, which has turned up fascinating artifacts and burials, but in chance and often isolated finds that generate as many questions as answers. The third is the burgeoning field of place-name analysis, which has centuries of linguistic interference to unravel, but offers compelling evidence for historical land use, occupation trends, and settlement patterns where it has been deployed. As I am a historian by trade, I focus my efforts in this chapter on the first form, but reference, and invite my readers to pursue more deeply, recent work on archeology and toponymy in the Isles.

The prevailing questions about these areas are *how* and *how much* they hosted and incorporated Norse-speaking settlers into the extant societies, if any. Simply put, we have little proof about whether these isles were uninhabited, or relatively recently inhabited by Middle Irish speakers (whether secular or clerical), or bearing populations that spoke languages that have no living descendants such as Pictish or Cumbric (the latter part of the same Celtic sub-family, however, as modern Welsh), before the Norse even arrived.

Modern understanding of ethnicity and linguistic movement has moved past the colonizer mindset of Victorian archeology, where every change in prevailing population or primary language was seen as due to intentional conquest and wholesale replacement. But, as there is no one universally accepted replacement for this mechanism—which is probably for the best, seeing the varieties of human change and adaptability even with robust documentation—it remains an art rather than a science to figure out what Norse-Gaelic cultural interchange was like in these places.

In addition to *how* and *how much*, it is also worth wondering *who* exactly was doing the movement: what class of people, or whole cross sections of society? From specific regions in what is now, say, western Norway or northern Denmark, or piecemeal from across Norse-speaking areas? And how would these populations have changed over time? The best information available is about the southernmost of these islands, the Suðreyjar, but even the term needs some clarification.

THE SUÐREYJAR

In English translations of medieval Icelandic settlement material, *suðreyskr* (adjective) and *Suðreyingr* (demonym, plural *Suðreyingar*) are both translated as "Hebridean." Indeed, modern Icelandic and Faroese use *Suðureyjar* and *Suðuroyggjar* respectively for the Inner and Outer Hebrides today. However, the medieval sense of Suðreyjar included the Isle of Man, islands of the Clyde, and some of western Scotland, potentially concealing the appearance of Manx and western Scottish contributions to the Gaelic character of Icelandic settlement. While I mostly follow already-published translations for this English-language book, I have retained "suðrey," which appears in the original, to ensure that I am not contributing to the conflation of the Hebridean archipelago with the rest of the Suðreyjar.

On the other side of the Norse-Gaelic interface, in Middle Irish the Hebrides are known with some spelling variations as *Inse Gall*, the Islands of the Foreigners. This persists into modern Irish and Scottish Gaelic, where they are *Innse Ghall* and *Innse Gall** respectively. "Gall" is a term for outsiders that originally came from Gaul,[2] but as shown by the Gall Gaidhel, it became an all-purpose term for non-Irish speakers and their ways.

Curiously, the twelfth-century text *Cellachâin* references the Innse Gall as the birthplace of the title character's love interest, Mór

*The title is ironic today, as the Hebrides have become a stronghold for Gaelic language usage in Scotland; perhaps instead of the "Islands of the Foreigners", they should be renamed *Innse Gàidhlig* ("Islands of the Gaels" in modern Scottish Gaelic)!

ingen Áedha mic Echu*. While married to a Norse-named husband who is son of another Norse-named man, Mór's father and grandfather both have names that are Gaelic; yet these men are explicitly kings of the "Innsi Gall"† and later specifically the "*innsi Fionnghall.*"[3] Either this is historical information that reveals an astonishingly early melding of Gaelic and Norse identity in tenth-century western Scotland, or as a fiction it implies a slippery lack of boundaries for the twelfth-century conception of Norse versus Gaelic identity two centuries prior. Either way, or somewhere between the two absolutes, *Cellacháin* demonstrates a softer division than "Gall" and "Gael" for Mór ingen Áedha, and this suggests the Suðreyjar was the first place that Norse-Gaelic culture came into being.

SUÐREYSKIR IN ICELAND: *LANDNÁMABÓK*

Many Gaelic settlers in *Landnámabók* (also known as *Landnáma*) are remembered as such, and the book of Icelandic land-taking (see chapter 4) also preserves their names. For instance, a settler named Helgi Bjóla is described as coming to Iceland directly from the Suðreyjar; his by-name is unknown in Norse and possibly comes from Irish *béal* for "mouth," both a piece of anatomy as well as the end of a river. "Kálman, a Suðreyskr by origin (*at ætt*)"[4] is likely the Norse approximation of Colmán, itself a diminutive of Colm. Kálman has a brother named Kylan (likely Cuileán[5]) whose son Kari "quarreled over an ox with Karli Konalsson of Karlastead, a freedman of Hrolfr of Geitland . . . Kari egged his slave into killing Karli."[6]

*Ingen means "daughter of" as mic is the genitive of "son of," as in Mór daughter of Áodh [himself] son of Eochaid.

†*Innsi* is the genitive or possessive form of the plural *Innse*, as they are kings of these islands.

This is a group of Gaels with distinctively ethnic names: Kari may be Corre or a similar Gaelic name, while Konal is almost certainly Conall. Figuring out which names were translated directly from Middle Irish into Old Norse, however, is a complicated process, particularly whether it occurred via bilingual writers who were aware of the original name and how to spell it, versus being written down by a writer who only knew how to render Norse (and Latin!) into written form.

In the recent *Norse-Gaelic Contacts in a Viking World*, the authors document the appearance of Gaelic names in early Icelandic texts and state the following below "*Konáll* < *Conall*":

> The name was current among [Icelandic] settlers from the late ninth century until the mid- to later eleventh. Oral transmission [from Irish to Norse] is likely, but *-u-* would better reflect the phonology of the first vowel. Marking *-a-* long does not accurately reflect original short *-a-*, nor can it mark stress which should fall on the first syllable. Doubling of *-ll* may be Old Norse nominal inflexion, rather than Gaelic orthography. . . .[7]

Were Kálman to have a Norse name, it would be suspected that he or his family had originated from overseas and lived in a Norse settlement in the Suðreyjar. However, his obviously Gaelic name, along with the names of his family, indicates strongly that he was a Gael; at the very least, for the author/compiler of *Landnáma*, some residents of the Suðreyjar used Gaelic names, even if they are incomprehensible to us today. Also interesting is that the son of a Suðreyskr has an enslaved person; to eleventh-century and perhaps even ninth-century Icelanders, the ability to own a bondsman did not depend on being a Norse-speaker from Scandinavia.

The next Suðreyskr in *Landnáma* is one Alfgeirr, who serves as a juryman at a "door court" and has a ship that is burnt in the chaos resulting from the trial.[8] Nothing is said of his personality or descendants. This Suðreyskr with a Norwegian name, and prestige in Iceland, is likely to have originated from Norway, or at the very least a Norse-speaking settlement in the Suðreyjar. A third Suðreyskr named Sæmundr is recorded as a partner in Viking raids,[9] and a fourth, named Bárðr, has no further information apart from his land-claim and descendants, though his name may indicate a Gaelic origin (see chapter 4).[10]

These mentions and characterizations of settlers from the Isles suggest that early Icelanders were comfortable and familiar with the inclusion of Suðreyskir in their country's history. Conversely, while the Færeyjar are mentioned a handful of times in *Landnáma*, and the Norðreyjar appear in the form of the Orkneyjar and a few mentions each of Hjaltland and Katanes, no one is described by the adjectival form of these lands. That is, settlers are described as passing through these areas, but never as *from* or descended from, using the word "ætt" for family or ancestry.

SUÐREYSKIR IN ICELAND: *LAXDÆLA SAGA*

Laxdæla Saga features an Irish slave who is discovered to be a noblewoman, and the story follows the lives of her son and grandson in Iceland. Not every Gael in *Laxdæla* is remembered fondly, however. A settler named Hrappr is "of Scottish descent (*skozkr að föðurætt*) on his father's side, but his mother's family had lived in the Hebrides, where he was born. A big, strong man, he was never willing to back down. . . . Most people cared little for Hrappr. He pushed his neighbors around. . . ."[11]

Hrappr's father is named as Sumarliði, a name derived from Old Norse for "summer traveler" (*sumar liði*) which was likely a poetic term for the rank-and-file Vikings. Sumarliði is still a first name in the Faroe Islands, and is celebrated in medieval and modern Scotland in the form of a twelfth-century folk hero named Somerled (*Somhairle* in Middle Irish, derived from the Norse and not meaning anything in Irish).

Why, if his father's family (*föðurætt*) was Scottish (*skozkr*), did Hrappr's father bear a Norse-derived name? The Scottish Somerled was presumably unrelated to this tenth-century Hrappr, but it is also possible that the name became attached to a Hebridean character when the saga was composed during or after Somerled's reign. A similar situation occurs with the Icelandic veneration of Kjarvalr Írakonungr, Cerball King of Ireland, who seems to be some kind of shorthand for Irish aristocracy rather than a single figure. Etchingham and colleagues conclude in a chapter that he "is just as likely a late, tendentious construct as other manifestations of the motif of prestigious Gaelic ancestry."[12]

Hrappr is also a very unusual name, only appearing elsewhere in Norse literature in *Ǫrvar-Odds Saga*, near the end of a list of men who serve as drinking buddies.[13] Hrappur is an approved male name in Iceland today but is used very infrequently, possibly because in the modern language *hrappur* means an imposter or cheat.

A whole family of sinister Suðreyskir is also found in *Laxdæla Saga*: "A man named Kotkel had only recently immigrated to Iceland, along with his wife, Grima and their sons . . . all of them skilled in witchcraft and accomplished magicians . . . their presence was anything but welcome."[14] Hrappr and Kotkel's family are remembered as nuisances who upset the social order with their powers, physical strength (even after death!) and supernatural skills.

While the Irish characters in *Laxdæla* are royal in some way or another, the Suðreyskir are common folk, even boorish. The difference between them may reflect a long-standing prejudice about settlers from Ireland, versus those from the Isles, in Iceland.

These Suðreyskir provide a sort of intermediary role in Icelandic settlement literature between people from Ireland and the Norse-speaking settlers, most of whom are believed to have come from what is now Norway. Their names and the names of their given ancestors combine Norse ones with ones that appear Middle Irish in origin, indicating that among the memory of Icelanders, the Suðreyskir were an ethnolinguistically mixed lot. This suggests, but does not prove, that a shared Norse-Gaelic society was taking shape there even before the late ninth-century settlement of Iceland. At the very least, for the twelfth- and thirteenth-century Icelanders who were partially a product of this fusion, the Suðreyjar were a crucible combining Norse and Irish speakers.

GAELS IN THE SUÐREYJAR

In his extraordinary book on the toponymy of Islay, one of the southernmost Hebrides, MacNiven acknowledges the pendulum swing in historiography back and forth between assumptions that entire populations were regularly and completely exterminated, versus gentler models where only social elites changed and the great bulk of the populace continued on without displacement. After discussing the merits and problems of these approaches, in terms of Islay, MacNiven posits a systematic genocide of Gaels by the Norse, aided by geography:

> The downfall of Islay's Dál Riatan [a Gaelic kingdom] society in this scenario would have been its island-based environment.

> Unlike the majority of predatory migrations . . . which took place in large continental districts where basic logistics may have hindered the progress of the aggressors or aided the resistance or escape of their victims, the fragmented insular landscape of the Hebrides offers no such checks. As a result, the scope for atrocity would have been magnified enormously. In this kind of insular environment, it would have been perfectly feasible for Norse fleets to surround individual islands and exterminate, round up or drive away entire populations before any help arrived.[15]

Hence the renaming of the Hebrides to Innse Gall, according to MacNiven. Yet, as shown by the Icelandic evidence, there were still plenty of Gaels and Irish speakers who were Suðreyskr. This can be accounted for by the inclusion of the Isle of Man among the Suðreyjar, and Manxmen among the people identified as Suðreyskir in Icelandic material. Mann is *Mön* in Old Norse, but the nearby island of Anglesey in Wales was also called *Mona* in Latin and *Môn* in Welsh, so sometimes there is confusion as to which landmass in the Irish Sea is being referred to in early medieval sources.

Located in sight of Northern Ireland, Scotland, northern England, and Wales simultaneously, the Isle of Man is both a natural crossing-space and contested battleground in the North Atlantic islands: "It is scarcely surprising that one medieval Welsh poet dubbed the Irish Sea 'Môr Manaw', 'the sea of Man'. . . the name of the island itself is derived from the Gaelic root *meadhon*, 'middle'."[16] The precise chronology and settlement pattern or patterns of the Manx witness to Norse incursions, both circa 800, and later after the reign of Godred Crovan (d. 1095), is not fully known. Current scholarship presumes that the Norse movement into the Isle of Man was either contemporaneous with eastern Ireland or directly parallel to Cumbrian settlement.[17] The archaeological evidence suggests a reality closer to that of Dublin, albeit a little later in time. This accords with slightly later politics, where the king of Dublin and Mann were often the same.[18]

But the actual mechanisms of this Norse takeover of, or social integration into, the Isle of Man are a scholastic gap that toponymic evidence can help to bridge. The established guide to the toponymy of the Isle of Man is Broderick's multivolume *Placenames of the Isle of Man*, which utilizes both oral material collected via the University of Mannheim Manx Place-Name Survey as well as written sources from the thirteenth through nineteenth centuries. Preliminary work on the interface of Norse and Gaelic place-names in the Isle of Man includes Fellows-Jensen's "Scandinavian Settlement in the Isle of Man and Northwest England: The Place-Name Evidence" from 1983, Wilson's "The Chronology of the Viking Age in the Isle of Man" (1998), Gammeltoft's "Scandinavian-Gaelic Contacts" (2004), and Broderick's "Goidelic-Scandinavian Language Contact in the Place-Names of the Isle of Man" (2007).

The fact is that Middle Irish, the precursor to modern Manx, was spoken in Isle of Man for centuries after the Norse arrived sometime in the eighth and ninth centuries. While Man is larger than Islay and thus more difficult to depopulate in such a way as MacNiven envisions above, it was nonetheless significantly changed by the Norse—and yet retained its cultural-linguistic character, as evidenced by the balance of place-names and the survival of its Gaelic language. The Middle Irish-speaking Manxmen contributed to the settlement of Iceland, and other excursions in the North Atlantic, as evidenced by the not uncommon appearance of Suðreyskir who were considered Irish, Scottish, and/or Gaelic by their "heritage (ætt)."

4
Gaels in the Settlement of Iceland

Iceland, isolated in the northern Atlantic Ocean, is nearly unique among the landmasses of the world in that its first human inhabitants arrived there soon before the reach of literacy to document it. It is just south of the Arctic Circle, though warmer than one might think due to the Gulf Stream, and experiences sustained volcanic activity from its location atop the Mid-Atlantic Ridge. Iceland's capitol city, Reykjavík, sets its founding at 874 CE with the establishment of Ingólfr Arnarson's farmstead there. There is both archeological and documentary evidence for some transient settlement before this, but ship technological advancement and the Medieval Warm Period were required to make Iceland permanently inhabitable in the ninth century.

The majority of settlers in Iceland were Norse speakers from Scandinavia, particularly Norway; but there was a significant number of Gaels among the population. The movement of Norse speakers from the Suðreyskir is covered in chapter 3, and there would have also been Norse speakers from Ireland and elsewhere in the Norse-speaking world outside Scandinavia. Many Irish-speaking

Gaels from Ireland and the Isles would have come to Iceland involuntarily as household slaves and concubines, but there were also not an insignificant number of people with Gaelic names or by-names in the record who were free settlers, or freed soon after arriving.

This is still encoded in modern Icelanders' genetics. In 2000 and 2001, Agnar Helgason and other geneticists analyzed the Y-chromosomes of 181 modern Icelandic men and the mitochondrial DNA of 401 Icelandic women. Presuming that the current population of Iceland bears a similar genetic makeup to its population at settlement—and medieval and early modern history does not show any significant immigration—the results are fascinating. While 80 percent of Icelandic men studied bore a Y-chromosome of Norwegian origin, 20 percent had one of Gaelic origin. Even more astounding, only 37 percent of the Icelandic women carried mtDNA of Norwegian origin; the remaining 63 percent bore Gaelic origin mtDNA. Not only was approximately forty percent of the settlement population from Ireland or Scotland, but a majority of women came from outside of Norway![1]

Generations after the settlement of Iceland, Christian Church-trained clerics produced vernacular historical tracts, poetry, and literature such as the *Eddas* and the *Íslendingasögur.* (The contemporary value of these texts is further explored in chapter 6.) Cultural assumptions, ranging from the vaguely nationalistic to the blatantly racist, have upheld these medieval documents as "purely Germanic" for centuries. Apart from the simple fact that North Atlantic literacy is an inherently Christian product and thus foreign, Iceland was never a solely *Norse* society. Rather, it was Norse-Gaelic from its start. The study of medieval Icelandic material is not a glimpse into a "Germanic" past, but rather a witness to an insular community that incorporated settlers from across the northwest of Europe.

EARLY ICELAND LITERARY MATERIAL

Landnámabók, the thirteenth century Book of settlements (lit. "land-naming"), records the populating and establishment of Iceland in the late ninth and tenth centuries. *Landnáma* begins by identifying Iceland with the "Thule" (*Týli*) mentioned by early English monk and scholar Bede (d. 735), and corroborates clerical knowledge of the island by the first Norse explorers' discovery of Christian men (*menn Kristni*) with Irish books (*bækr írskar*) and other religious objects. These *papar* ("fathers"?) are described as having come from west over the ocean (*verit vestan um haf*) and are explained as *Vestmenn*, "Men from the West."*

Our modern conception of geography would, of course, argue that Ireland is technically to the south-south*east* of Iceland. But in a world before compasses and latitudes, Iceland was more conceived as the northern height of an equilateral triangle with what is now Norway to the eastern point and Ireland at the western point. The Gaels were Vestmenn to the Norse mindset, regardless of where they existed in an objective geographical sense.

At the end of the version of *Landnáma* believed to have been written by Sturla Þórðason (d. 1284), the composer reports:†

> According to well-informed people some of the settlers of Iceland were baptized, mostly those who came from <u>west over</u>

*Compare this with Ostmen, "Men from the East," what Norse-speaking residents of Dyflin called themselves for generations: see chapter 1.

†Underline mine.

> the ocean [*er kómu vestan um haf*]. . . . Some of them kept up their Christianity [*sumir vel kristni*] till they died, but in most families this didn't last, for the sons of some built temples [*reistu hof*] and made sacrifices [*blótuðu*], and [Ice]land was completely heathen for a hundred winters [*alheiðit nær hundraði vetra*].[2]

In his book on Icelandic history, Jón Jóhannesson writes, "Although the majority of the colonists of Iceland were pagan, their beliefs were of two different kinds. On the one hand there was the belief in *landvættir* (guardian spirits of the country); on the other, there was *goðatrú* or *ásatrú* (the faith in the gods)."[3] To this, Turville-Petre replies:

> I would not wish to assert that this opinion is correct, but we can safely say that the belief in the lower beings was considerably more persistent than the belief in gods. Even today, many people both in Iceland and other western lands believe in fairies or 'hidden people,' even trolls and such-like elemental beings. Belief in these lower beings is not inconsistent with orthodox Christianity; it hardly concerns Christianity.[4]

A modern Icelandic highway was famously rerouted so as to avoid knocking down a troll-stone,[5] paralleling the modern Irish concern with preserving "fairy-forts" (*ráthanna*).[6] As nature spirit beliefs have persisted to the twentieth century, clearly they were still a factor in twelfth- and thirteenth-century Iceland.

The settlers were not just heathen and Christian, with a clear delineation between the two categories. There were those who worshipped the landvættir and those who worshipped a specific god or gods, those who saw Christ as one of their gods, and even those who did not worship anything. There are also many figures who are described as sorcerers or shape-shifters; and there are just as many men as women, and as many "good" people as "bad," with these talents. The *nature* of Icelandic magical practices is also not essential to this discussion, but it serves as a barometer for early medieval Icelanders' opinion on the number, quality, and personality of magic-workers and their relationship with Gaels at settlement.

What is remarkable is that modern readers know this today from medieval documents, from the hand of Christianized scribes. Unlike many other cultures who demonized their ancestors' pre-Christian traditions, Icelanders instead cherished their preliterate customs by recording them for posterity in the *Eddas*. Snorri rationalized his composition of heathen beliefs by turning the gods into Trojan heroes who came to Norway and became deified over the centuries.[7] A similar "sanitization" of heathen mythology is found in the twelfth-century Irish tale *Colloquy of the Sages* (*Acallam na Senórach*), where two ancient god-heroes meet Saint Patrick, become baptized, and are then allowed to tell their tale_indeed, Patrick is *encouraged* by angels to record their pagan antics.[8]

The *Poetic Edda* does not have a central narrative and thus no voice to avert suspicion. It is distinctly subversive, particularly the poems "*Völuspá*" and "*Hávamál*," the former an explicit and unapologetic description of heathen cosmology, and the latter a collection of proverbs clearly pre-Christian in origin. The stories in the *Poetic Edda* evoke the short prose stories from eighth-century Ireland that remember the gods without any Christian interruption, such as "The Sickness of Cú Chulainn" (*Serglige Cón Chulainn*) and

"The Wooing of Étaín" (*Tochmarc Étaín*).[9] These Irish stories and the *Eddas* were composed in the vernacular, a celebration both of pre-Christian traditions and of linguistic identity.

Landnáma suggests that Icelanders who were Christian had come from "west over the sea." Generally, scholars assume that this was true in the reverse; Ireland and Scotland had been Christian countries for centuries, thus all Gaels captured in the eighth and ninth centuries were Christian. This is not necessarily true, however. As demonstrated by the modern reverence for ráthanna mentioned above, pre-Christian traditions have very long lives in Ireland. The number of Gaelic sorcerers is small but notable in the early medieval Iceland sources.

If Iceland was pagan for a hundred years, as *Landnám* states, what happened to the children of Christian Gaelic settlers? Some scholars have suggested that they maintained their religion and eased the conversion of Iceland to Christianity in the year 999 or 1000 CE. However, descriptions of the conversion of Iceland are remarkably cool and neutral, and it is emphasized that it was a prudent political conversion decided by logical debate rather than an impassioned religious frenzy. Is it not more likely that most of the Icelanders of Gaelic descent became heathen themselves?

"It seems that, when the settlement of Iceland began, people were very liberal about religious belief."[10] The question is more if these un-churched people of Gaelic descent worshipped their contemporaries' gods of Norse origin and the landvættir that they brought from Scandinavia, or those of their ancestors from Ireland, Scotland, and the Isles? This is further explored with a specific example later in this chapter, but let us look at some documents of the settlement to get an idea of how Gaels and Norse-Gaels in Iceland were remembered.

LANDNÁMABÓK

Landnám acknowledges the Irish papar but does not comment on their religion. However, the story about Hjörleifr and Ingólfr Arnarson, Iceland's first settlers, encodes a morality tale. Ingólfr offers a great sacrifice (*a blóti miklu*) but Hjörleifr refuses to participate. Later, when Hjörleifr is dishonorably slain by the men from Ireland, whom he had taken in slavery, Ingólfr dryly comments, "in my experience, this is what always happens to people who won't hold sacrifices (*ef eigi vill blóta*)."[11] While Hjörleifr is disgraced in death, Ingólfr is celebrated as Iceland's first settler, and also as a pious heathen: he is honoring the "wrong" gods, of course, but for the Christian composer of *Landnáma*, performing blót well is better than doing nothing.

Several entries later, another settler is given a more explicit endorsement, despite his heathen nature: "Þorkell Moon (*Món*) . . . gave himself to the god who created the sun (*guði er sólina hafði skapat*). He had led a life as blameless (*hreinliga*) as the best of Christians."[12] In the *Acallam na Senórach*, it is stressed that the characters who had died before Christianity arrived in Ireland were yet proto-Christians who had adhered to a Christian model of virtue. Just as the Irish author of the *Acallam* stressed that native traditions were worth transmitting because of their inherent virtue, the Icelandic scribe of *Landnám* retained a memory—or created a fiction—of clean-living heathens who were not Christian, only because they had not heard of it yet.

Similarly, the eleventh-century Irish Cerball of Osraige saga found ways to excuse Norse heathens in Ireland. The Danair, led by Horm, operate as proto-Christians who offer war-booty to Saint Patrick for advantage in battle against the Lochlannaigh. In her

2004 article, Downham explores the role of heathen Norse factions considered closer or further to Christianity in the Osraige chronicle, categorizing the Danair as "unpleasant but useful to Irish kings," "semi-Christian," and thus the *least* bad* as allies for the Gaels.[13] Their sacrifices of gold and silver to Patrick (*do ór da thabhairt do Pádraicc*) as well as their abstention "from meat and from women for a while, for the sake of piety (*ar chrabhudh*)" result in an unlikely victory for them "by the grace of Patrick (*cosgan tria rath Padraicc*)."[14]

Holy Land in Landnáma

An earth-based religion, such as that practiced in Norway and Iceland in the tenth century, values dirt from a sacred region as imbued with holiness. It is similar to the medieval Catholic concept of the saint's relic, except that natural objects rather than body parts serve as the focus for worship and conduit to the divine. The Christian concept of consecrated earth was a concern for early Icelanders who did not have churches to be buried in, resulting in some ingenious methods of holy burial: the Christian Auðr the Deep-Minded (*djúpúðga*), for example, was buried at the high tide mark.[15]

> Hrappr . . . had a son called Örlygr whom he gave in fosterage to the Holy Bishop Patrick† of the Suðreyjar. He had a great desire to go to Iceland. . . . The bishop provided him with church timber (*kirkuvið*), an iron bell, a plenarium, and consecrated earth

*See chapter 2 for the differences between Danair and Lochlannaigh in Irish material.

†No bishops named Patrick are known from this time, and this is likely referencing the saint as an "appropriate" name for a Christian Gael. However, few saints' names alone were used as personal names in Old and Middle Irish, rather names with elements like *Máel-* and *Gille-* meaning "servant of."

> (*mold vígða*) which Örlygr was to place beneath the corner posts of his church.[16]

Here we see a Christian expected to carry earth across the North Atlantic to bring sanctity to Iceland. Compare it with a non-Christian Icelander who did the same:

> Þórhaddr the Old was a temple priest (*hofgóði*) at Mæri in Þrándheimr [in Norway]. He had a great desire to go to Iceland, but before he set off, he dismantled the temple and took the pillars and some earth from under the temple (*hofsmoldina*) with him. He put in at Stǫðvarfjǫrðr, and declared the whole fjord sacred (helgi), just as his place in Mæri had been.[17]

The difference between consecrated and unconsecrated earth was a priest's blessing; it was not a transitive property. Why would Örlygr's bishop send him to Iceland with consecrated earth to put under the corners of the church, in much the same way as the heathen priest Þórhaddr sanctified his temple? If a mistake was made, it seems much more likely that the Christian authors would confuse a heathen ritual for a Christian one, rather than the other way around. Was this how monks from Iona consecrated land, in a suspiciously heathen manner? Were the Christian authors making a subtle dig at the Gaels by implying that their Christian rituals were the same as heathen ones?

If so, it seems no real insult, as the description of heathen practices abound in *Landnám*, particularly that of landscape veneration. The surprising story of Seal-Þórir involves a merman, a prophecy concerning a mare, and a preternatural vision of a volcanic eruption. His story ends with, "When they died, Seal-Þórir and his pagan kinsmen (*frændr . . . heiðnu*) went into Þórisbjörg."[18] The descendants of Auðr djúpúðga "lost their faith (*spilltist trúa*)" and "believed they would go into the hills when they died."[19]

Belief in the landvættir was also strong, as *Landnáma* can attest. One entry reads: "People with second sight could see that all the guardian spirits of the land accompanied Hafur-Björn when he attended the Alþing, and [his brothers] Þorstein and Þord when they went out fishing." The entry immediately following states, "Ölvir Eysteinsson took possession of land east of Gríms River where no one had dared to settle for fear of land-spirits (*landvættum*), since Hjörleifr was killed there" by his Irish-born slaves early in the settlement.[20] Note that this implies that the murder had riled up the landvættir already extant—or attracted new ones, perhaps including part of the unfortunate Hjörleifr!

Landnáma talks casually about "second sight" in several locations, usually referring to the sight of shape-shifters in their spiritual form. It is hard to describe what second sight is, but it appears to be an ability to see or sense an otherwise invisible spirit or being. To a modern skeptic, there is no difference between the ability to see a visiting spirit and the ability to physically change into an animal, both being equally impossible; but to medieval Icelanders the former was an actual skill: "While literary scholars . . . tend to regard dreams, hauntings, and other such 'bizarre' phenomena as literary devices rather than social realities . . . events that seem fantastic to us do not seem fantastic to other people . . . they may, in fact, be aspects of their culturally constituted realities."[21]

Dufþak (Irish Dubthach)[22] of Dufþaksholt is described in *Landnáma* as both a "mighty shape-changer (*hamrammr mjök*)" and also a freed slave (*leysingi*). By his name and freed status he is clearly

Irish, but he is also a shape-changer! *Landnáma* gives an account of a supernatural fight he participated in:

> Stórólfr [Hængsson] lived at Hváll, and he and Dufþak quarreled over grazing. One evening, about sunset, someone with second sight (*ófreskr*) noticed a huge bear set out from Hváll, and a bull from Dufþaksholt. They met at Stórólfsvöllr and set upon one another in a fury, the bear getting the best of it. In the morning, people saw there was a hollow where they had met, and it was just as if the earth had been turned upside down. . . . Both men were badly hurt.[23]

Shape-shifters dot the landscape of Icelandic literature, and are presented matter-of-factly throughout the medieval period. This passage hints at their "true" nature; not people actually altering their physical form, but spiritual animals that could only be seen by people with special skill who could move and interact with other spiritual animals.

These forms were either the spiritual appearance of their mind separated from their body, or else their "fetch" (*fylgja*). The fylgja is a complicated aspect of Icelandic folklore and, in brief, appears to be a guardian or attendant spirit attached to every person from birth and intimately linked with the physical afterbirth.[24] In short, when shape-shifters appear in the literature, we should not discard them as pure fantasy or fiction, as they were as real as anything else to the medieval Icelanders who recorded them.

Christianity in Landnáma

Turville-Petre remarks that among the early Icelanders, "Some thought that belief in Þórr was not inconsistent with the Christian faith." The epitome of this observation is Helgi the Lean (*inn magri*), a settler whose mother was from Ireland, and who himself grew up in the Suðreyjar. "Helgi's faith was very much mixed (*blandinn mjök í trú*): he believed in Christ (*trúði á Krist*) but invoked Þórr when it came to voyages and difficult times (*hét á Þór til sjófara ok harðræða*)."[25]

The polytheist pre-Christian religion of the Icelanders was not just the belief in a plurality of certain gods, but rather the *belief* in all gods everywhere, and individual *devotion* to one or a small number of them. The figure of Christ preceded Christian monotheism into northern Europe. Until Iceland converted en masse and got the "full message," Christ was seen as one of countless deities throughout the world who could be worshipped at the choice of the devotee.

Helgi's Irish mother "Raförta"* should have taught him better—or perhaps, she was not a monotheist Christian herself. It is not beyond the improbable that as an Irish royal woman, Raförta and her family had retained Irish polytheist religious traits. Kingship in Ireland was intimately connected with the land and therefore all the ancient, pre-Christian nature-based traditions bound up in it. For example, in the seventh-century Irish text *Lives of St. Patrick*, a pagan king named Loegaire allows Patrick to proselytize in his kingdom, but refuses to accept baptism himself. After his death, Loegaire is required to be buried upright in his armor, facing his people's enemies, so that he can serve as their guardian even in death. This kingly burial is also reminiscent of previously covered stories in *Landnáma* where Icelandic heathens believe in an afterlife spent underground.

This early medieval record of the settlement of Iceland is full

*This atypical name is neither Norse nor clearly Gaelic, though it is possibly a feminized form of Irish *Robartach*. Etchingham et al., *Norse-Gaelic Contacts*, 310–11.

of Christians, heathens, sorcerers, and people who were somewhere in between. There are also three entries of people whose epithet was "the Godless," who "believed in their own strength and refused to hold sacrifices."[26] Recall the untimely, dishonorable demise of Hjörleifr, who also refused to honor the gods. Apparently, being a self-assured atheist was the only religious transgression to the compiler of *Landnáma*.

HEATHENISM IN *EGILS SAGA*

Egils Saga is a remarkable saga for its casual portrayal of heathen practices and beliefs. Figures throughout the saga have extraordinary talents and abilities, and are yet treated as normal people with mundane problems. The eponymous hero and many of his associates demonstrate a great aptitude for magic of various types. It is believed that the author of *Egils* may be none other than Snorri Sturluson.[27] If this is true, it is possible that he used the saga as a complement to the *Prose Edda* as a showcase for heathenism in action.

"Skallagrímr [Egil's father] . . . chose the strongest and boldest (*sterkastir at afli ok hraustastir*) of his men and neighbors to go with him . . . [including] the brothers Þorbjörn Hunchback (*krumr*) and Þórðr Hobbler (*beigaldi*). They were known as Þorörna's sons—she lived near Skallagrímr and was a sorceress (*fjölkunnig*)."[28] Note that the brothers are both named for their debilitating deformities, and yet Skallagrímr considers them of the "strongest and boldest." It is possible that they inherited or learned sorcery from their mother to make up for their physical disabilities. If they are known as Þorörna's sons, then they value her name over the name of their father and term themselves such, an important note to make while considering identity.

"In all there were twelve in the party, all outstandingly powerful men, and many of them were shape-shifters. . . . '[T]hey are more like giants than human beings in size and appearance.'"[29] The unusual abilities and appearance of these men may indicate a relationship between physical appearance and spiritual or psychic power. The hero of the tale, who has not been born yet at this point in the narrative, is known for his ugliness as well as his intelligence. It is a common association in traditional cultures, including Ireland. Deformity is associated with sinister magic in stories of the *Fomori* ("under-horrors") and other Irish tales, while ancient pagan heroes of Ireland are described as gigantic in comparison to modern or contemporary people.[30] It seems to be that people who appear strange are considered to think or act strangely as well, a common medieval literary motif of the outside appearance echoing the inner self.

But not only people with deformities or unnatural height possess the ability to do witchcraft in *Egils*:

> Gunnhildr was outstandingly attractive and wise, and well versed in the magic arts (fjölkunnig mjök) . . .
>
> Þorgeirr was very wealthy, he made many sacrifices to the gods and was well versed in the magic arts (*blótmaðr mikill ok fjölkunnigr*). . . .
>
> Skallagrímr had a servant woman (*ambátt*) named Þorgerðr Brák. . . . She was an imposing woman, as strong as a man and well versed in the magic arts (fjölkunnig mjök).[31]

Gunnhildr, Þorgeirr, and Þorgerðr are all upstanding characters within *Egils*, and the author must have been making the point that knowing sorcery was common in Skallagrím's time. The repeated term "fjölkunnig" means, literally, "many-knowledged," but as evidenced by its descendant, modern Icelandic *fjölkynnig*, the term specifically refers to magic usage or sorcery.

In this multitude of fjölkunnigsfolk, Þorgerðr Brák is of great interest to Norse-Gaelic paganism. "Brák" is from Old Irish *brecc*, freckled, suggesting Þorgerðr the ambátt is an Irish sorceress. The deformity–magical skill relationship arises again with the term "brecc." While seen as quintessentially Irish today, freckles were unattractive in early medieval Ireland, and "brecc" has the connotation of "spotted" or "marked."[32] Þorgerðr Brák is thus a symbol of the crossroads between Gaelic and Norse heathenism, as a heathen woman from a nominally Christian land.

Norse-Gaelic Heathenry in Other Sagas

"Heathen were the people of Greenland at that time."[33] "Greenland had been converted to Christianity by that time, although Eirik the Red (*rauðr**) had died before the conversion."[34] "In those days Christianity was still in its infancy in Greenland."[35] During the course of *Grœnlendinga Saga* and *Eiríks Saga Rauða*, a mass conversion occurs in Greenland in a bloodless and logical movement similar to that of Iceland. It was politically motivated, as the king of Norway, Olaf Tryggvason, was a devout Christian and anyone who wanted to gain power in the North Sea had to be his ally and thus Christian. This saga speaks about Greenlanders as a unit without examining the individuals involved and uses the conversion as a conventional chronological marker.

Early in the saga is a remarkable passage about a woman named Þorbjörg, the "Little Prophetess," and her visit to Herjolfsnes in Greenland. She is a fortune-teller and spends "the winter visiting,

**Rauðr*, *rauði*, and *rauða* are all forms of the Old Icelandic word meaning "red."

one after another, farms to which she had been invited, mostly by people curious to learn their own future or what was in store for the upcoming year." A detailed description of her costly and unusual wardrobe is written, continuing the theme of unusual appearance connected with witchcraft. She is clearly well-paid for her services, which are depicted as true and useful rather than the work of a charlatan.

> She asked for women who knew the chants required for carrying out magic rites, which are called ward songs [*varðlokkur*]. . . . Guðriðr answered, "I have neither magical powers nor the gift of prophecy, but in Iceland my foster-mother, Halldís, taught me chants she called ward songs."

At first Guðriðr is hesitant to help Þorbjörg, as she is a Christian. However, she is persuaded by her husband to assist Þorbjörg and "spoke the chant so well and so beautifully that people there said they had never heard anyone recite in a fairer voice."[36] The ritual is a success and Þorbjörg receives prophetic messages from disembodied "spirits." Guðriðr had learned the songs from her foster mother who was presumably heathen (Halldís was deceased at this time) and remembers them despite having become a Christian. She also performs the songs and receives a prophecy despite her conversion. This passage suggests both that the conversion was not sharply defined, as well as that women were remembered to play critical roles in magical rites.

There is a brief but interesting passage towards the end of the *Vatnsdæla* saga where a magic user is called upon at a prearranged duel to clear the weather, which is implied to have been cast rather than naturally occurring:

> . . . on that journey the weather turned foul, and they believed it was a witches' storm (*gerningaveðr*, lit. "induced/performed weather/storm").
>
> There was a man named Bárðr. . . . They asked him to call off the bad weather (*hann af taka veðrið*), because he had the wisdom of a magician (*margkunnigr*). He asked them to join hands and make a circle (*handkrækjast og gera hring*); he then went round backwards three times, spoke in Irish (*mælti írsku*), and bade them all say "yes" out loud (*"já" við kveða*)—and this they did. He then waved a kerchief (*giska*) at the mountain and the weather relented.[37]

While this Bárðr is not introduced or explained elsewhere, his name may suggest a connection with Ireland, or Norse-Gaels living there, as there is a Bárith in *Cerball*,[38] suggesting at least one Norse operator in Ireland with the name. It is also not dissimilar to Old Irish "bard," same as in modern English, meaning a poet and often with magical connotations. Bárðr is called upon and delivers, and the method of his magic is explicitly spoken in Irish. For the author and audience of the *Vatnsdæla* saga, when strange magical weather looms, call on an Irish-speaker for relief.

CONCLUSIONS

This is far from an exhaustive list of Irish or Gaelic appearances in early medieval Icelandic literature, but hopefully serves as a *pars pro toto* that the material is full of them. Scholars' presumptions that all settlers from Ireland or other nominally Christian regions would have kept up their religion in Iceland has colored interpretation by assuming that anything magical or pagan in the narratives must have come from Scandinavia or other unconverted areas. But cultural fusion and the revival of pre-Christian Gaelic beliefs were already well underway by the time of Icelandic settlement, as evidenced by material found in other chapters of this book. Norse-Gaelic religion was as much a part of Icelandic identity as religion straight from Scandinavia or other Germanic-speaking lands.

5
Norse Heathenism in Irish Dynastic Narratives

The story of Norse speakers' arrival into and interaction with Gaelic Ireland is preserved in Middle Irish dynastic propaganda written in support of a contemporary ruler by portraying his ancestor's valiant triumph over the Vikings. This preserves the medieval Gaelic perception of their own history concerning the Vikings, which reveals their perceived relationship with the descendants of those Vikings in Ireland, the Hiberno-Norse.

After the Cambro-Norman invasion of 1169 CE, Irish literature becomes fraught with the weight of invasion and conquest; in short, it becomes the story of the colonized. This darkens and clouds the history of the Vikings, who become proto-Normans and colonizers themselves in the literature. Texts composed before 1169 show a more nuanced view of the Norse in Ireland. Here, they speak a different language and operate using different technology and living patterns than the Gaels; yet they intermarry the elites in willing exchange, join their dynastic struggles and territorial disputes, and bring innovation and wealth to Ireland.

Three of the most famous Middle Irish dynastic propaganda

texts from this period include the reconstructed Cerball of Osraige saga (shortened to *Cerball*) preserved in the fourth section of the Fragmentary Annals of Ireland. This was composed for Donnchad mac Gilla Patráic,[1] who "extended his sway over the province of Leinster in the 1030s, and he may have desired to control the wealthy viking-towns on the coast of that province" by using his illustrious ancestor Cerball mac Dúnlainge and his power over the Norse as historical precedent.[2] The largest and most well-known of the texts is the *Cogadh Gáedhel re Gallaibh* or "War of the Gael Against the Foreigners" (shortened to *Cogadh*)[3] which was composed in the early twelfth century for a descendant of Brian Bóru mac Cénnetig to glorify this ancestor.[4] Finally, the *Caithréim Chellacháin Chaisil* (shortened to *Cellacháin*) was composed as a "riposte" to *Cogadh*, essentially functioning as a fan-written prequel for the benefit of the Mac Carthaigh dynasty.[5]

Rather than attempt to identify the signifiers of heathenism in these sources as genuine worship or practice, this chapter considers the eleventh- and early twelfth-century Gaelic imagination of what the Norse speakers in Ireland would have done as part of their ethnolinguistic culture. Masculinity and the concept of honor (*enech* in Irish, *menskr* in Norse) is also deeply entwined with their worldview. This is not what the Vikings in Ireland "believed," but what the Gaelic, Irish-speaking authors of these texts imagined the ancestors of their Hiberno-Norse neighbors believed. Nonetheless there are certainly kernels of truth planted here in the fertile ground of imagination.

HEATHEN PERSPECTIVES IN IRISH CONCEPTS

Several themes emerge in the sources as to how the heathen Norse functioned. *Cerball* includes dialogue from Horm, a Danar* leader,

**Danar* is the singular form of *Danair*.

to his men before battle, which hints at a cohesive albeit military worldview:

> What you must do now is to go single-mindedly (*go h-aon-meanmnach*) against them, as if you did not expect to live, but were not waiting for death either; and revenge yourselves.
>
> And though you may not have a lucky victory (*cosgar sainmheach*) thereby, we will have done what our gods (*ar n-dee*) and our fate (*ar toicthe*) will give to us. . . .[6]

For Horm and his men, the fighting itself is honorable and their "gods" and "fate" determine the outcome, rather than whether or not they are victorious. To the Gaelic audience, the Danair are fanatically "single-minded" where they do not even care about the outcome but that they fight as if they are "not waiting for death." These Danair are dangerous for their devotion to warfare without the mitigation of their "gods," whereas the Gaelic Irish fight with the Christian god in mind.

Later in the saga, a pitched battle in the area of Kildare sees Áed Finnliath mac Néill fighting a combined army of Flann mac Sinna, the Gaelic Laighin (Leinstermen), and Norse Lochlannaigh. Áed's rally before the battle is the Christian counterpoint to Horm's heathen call before:

> It is not by the number of warriors that a battle is won, but by the help of God (*fhurtacht an Coimdheadh*) and by the righteousness of a sovereign. Arrogance and excessive size of an army, moreover, are not what God values, but rather humble bearing and firmness of heart. . . . When you see me rising, rise, all of you, together against them, as God will guide you (*faillseachus Día dhuibh*).[7]

The use of "gentiles" (*gentes*) demarcates the Norse as non-Christian, and this manifests in further Old Testament imagery of the Norse performing "idolatry" (*iodhaladhradh*). Áed instructs his men to "spare the Christians and attack the idolators" (*legidh dona Criostadhibh 7 imridh for iodhaladharthaibh*),[8] distinguishing the Gaelic Laighin and Norse Lochlannaigh despite their military allegiance.

MILITARY MASCULINITIES

These are dynastic propaganda narratives written to ennoble a valiant ancestor to the point of heroism. Therefore warfare and martial prowess are constant themes, but the language used to describe Gaels and Norse in combat differ strikingly. Gaels are accorded bravery and acclaim by leaping into battle wearing fine linen and beautifully decorated accessories, indicating that their power is from their athleticism and fearlessness. The Norse, on the other hand, are described as heavily armored in metal helmets and coats of mail, and move slowly and brutally in shielded formations. This reflects on the Gaelic conception of how the Norse see battle and warfare from their heathen perspective(s).

The historical reality of ninth and tenth century military activity is not what is being described in the literature, it is important to warn. The archaeology of northern European warfare is poorly attested in the first place; for instance, a single helmet survives from the whole of the Old Norse-speaking region during the "Viking Era." Common sense also suggests that combatants would utilize whatever arms and armor they could afford. Even if Norse technology outstripped that of the landed Irish at first, surely the Gaels would rapidly engage in trade and other methods to obtain equipment.

Rather, these narratives capture the eleventh- and early twelfth-century imagination of Viking battles in Ireland. For the Middle Irish audience, the conflict of their ancestors was characterized by the different fighting styles of Norse and Gael, and the respective societies' differing views on masculinity and honor (enech/menskr).

The *Cogadh* describes the Norse oppression of the province of Munster, as synecdoche for all Ireland, in almost entirely masculine language, particularly against the feminine Munster/Ireland: ". . . they spread themselves over Mumhain; and they built Dúns, and fortresses, and landing-ports, over all Erinn . . . so that they made spoil-land, and sword-land, and conquered-land of her (. . . *co ndernsat ferann creiċe, ocus cloidim, ocus forgaḃala go foirleṫan, ocus go coitċenn [di]*)" (underline mine).[9]

It states that the Vikings have displaced every Gaelic Irish king, chief, abbot, steward, and soldier (i.e., replacing the man of the house), reducing agency "so that none of the men of Erinn had power (*co nach raibhe a comas ag aen duine dferaibh Erenn*)" to provide hospitality or defend his family or people.[10] The alliterative language literally reads "any people of the men (-feraibh) of Ireland," emphasizing the depersonalization of the men by the loss of their leadership roles. The author explicitly attributes the Norse triumph to their coats of mail (*lurech*), swords (*claidium*), and spears (*sleag*), as well as "their strength, and their venom, and their ferocity (*a neirt, a nemi, ocus a nbadamlacht*)."[11]

Much later in the narrative, the Norse forces gathered for the Battle of Clontarf are described as two thousand men all wearing full-body metal armor of some kind:

> And there was not one villain or robber of that two thousand Norse (danar) gathered for Clontarf who had no polished, strong

> triple-plated, glittering armour of refined iron, or of cool uncorroding brass, encasing their sides and bodies from head to foot (*o cennaib co bondaib*).[12]

"Blue/grey people (*Daeine glasa*)" and "foreigners of the armor (*goill na luireach*)" further equivocate the Norse with their coats of mail.[13]

Cellachâin continues this imagery, describing the forces of Amlaib as "a thick, dark stronghold of black iron, and a grey-polished, hard-sharp city of battle-shields, and a strong enclosure of stout shafts(*dún dluith duaibhsech duibh-iarainn ⁊ cathair clogudghlas cruaghfhaebrach chaithsciath ⁊ ruadhbhuaili rembarcrann*)."[14] This conflates the armored Norse with their fortified towns, another fundamental difference in lifestyle from the Gaels in Ireland. A fictional battle at Ard Macha portrays the Norse as "a glittering, death-bringing *booley* of combatants (*cathbhuaili crithrech chombartach*),"[15] and later at Dún Dealgan, "a dense fortress of dark shields, and an immovable oakwood of venomous and strong spears (*dun dighain doinnsciathach ⁊ sluaghdhoire sesmach slegh neimhnech nertchalma*)."[16]

The Gaels, in opposition, are depicted as heroically charging into battle without regard for bodily protection. Within *Cogadh*, Brian Boru and his brother Mathgamhain take different approaches to the Viking incursions: the latter makes truces and cedes land to the Norse in order to save his people, while the former attacks them relentlessly and gets nearly all of his followers killed. Brian chides his brother for making compromises and losing honor, while Mathgamhain believes that his responsibility is for his subjects' lives rather than valor. These two exemplars of Gaelic masculinity show literary tension between battle glory and protection of their charges, in the pursuit of ideal manhood.

Eventually, Brian convinces Mathgamhain that the long-term survival of their family relies on the eradication of the Norse, and they go into warfare together. In order to have any chance, they have to recruit other Gaelic families, only one of which is described as "having a large warrior's shield at his side." The very call to arms acknowledges that it is "unequal warfare (*nanforran*)";[17] it is the valor (enech) and manliness of Gaelic masculinity that calls them to fight even against the odds, rather than being seen as a foolish suicide.

This eventually results in Clontarf, of course, where the author waxes effusively about Brian's forces and allies: "the stainless intelligent heroes of the Gaidhil along with them (*geratai glangasta goedel ar oen riu*)."[18] This description of their weaponry and battle strategy comes later in the chapter, with emphasis on their cloth tunics and vests. Shields and helmets are only "on the heads of chiefs and royal knights" and seem much more decorative than functional, being made of gold and gems. Surprisingly, their armory includes "Lochlann axes," but they are specifically "in the hands of chiefs and leaders" and only for "cutting and maiming the close well-fastened coats of mail (*fri tuarcain lureaċ lutmar drulineċ dib*)."[19] The leaders are also the only ones with swords.

This is an eye-catching array of men, but their weapons are less formidable than the skills with which they wield them. Brian's son Murchad is described as the height of masculine ideal and "the last man in Erinn who had equal dexterity in striking [with a sword] with his right and with his left hand."[20] He uses this skill to break the impenetrable Norse armor at "the buttons, and the fastenings, and the clasps, and the buckles that were fastening the helmet (*. . . na cnaip, ocus cengal, ocus iata, ocus na coraigthi barat ic congbail in cathbairr . . .*)."[21] Murchad also pulls the mail coat off of another

Norseman and then wrestles him, dramatically stabbing him with his own sword three times![22]

Cellachâin makes the difference between the Gaels and Norse even more explicit, stating that the Gaels do not have armor but only fancy clothing. Undaunted, in battle they "put the hooks of their shields over each other, and they made 'champion-knots' (*snadman[n]a niadh*) by attaching their broad belts to each other."[23] But the Norse slaughter the Gaels due to their lack of armor. This causes the hero Cellachán to reach a new fury and somehow overpower his technological disadvantage, inciting the rest of his men to attack with renewed violence focused on the Norse outside of their coats of mail. For example, one puts "his spear through the boss of the buckler and beneath the rim of the helmet into the [Norse] hero, so that it passed quickly into the hero's neck," and another performs a maneuver where he pulls up a Norseman's coat of mail and disembowels him.[24] The Gaels carry this brutal style of no-holds-barred fighting to Dún Dealgan, a ship-borne battle (see chapter two), where they use the weight of the mail-coats against the Norse by overloading their ships and throwing them overboard to drown.

These narratives explore the literary boundaries between Norse and Gaelic performative masculinity, where Norse warfare is inelegant and brutish to the Gaels, and Gaelic warfare is poorly arranged and underpowered in the sight of the Norse. The best evidence of how these men occupy different standards occurs when they cross boundaries and the author demonstrates how a change has overcome them. When the Munster forces go to fight for Cellachán with naval warfare, they must transition from Gaels to Norse in their tactics, and to their very appearance and mindset: "the senses, and feelings, and thoughts of the heroes underwent a change . . ."[25] In this literature no such transformation is ever shown for a woman, whose domain is off the battlefield and whose sociolinguistic allegiance is fluid. To be a man in pre-Norman Ireland, one must choose a side by which to measure his masculinity.

CROSSING THE BOUNDARIES OF NORSE AND GAEL

The *Cerball* saga has several mentions of the Gall Gaidhel, the Foreign Gaels first mentioned in the introduction to this book. But viewed in the context of this dual avenue of masculinity in pre-Norman Ireland, their role is clear: they are men of Irish origin (*Eireannaigh*) who have voluntarily adapted to the Norse mode of masculine gender performance. The annalist explains that they are *daltaí* of the Norse, a term that refers to the formal institution of fosterage but also connotes students and apprentices, indicating that they have learned from the Northmen (Normannaigh), "and sometimes they are even called normannaigh." For the annalist, these men who have taken on Norse methods of warfare are idiots (*scuit*) for having given up their patrimony, a similar sentiment expressed by Brian to Mathgamhain in *Cogadh*, and furthermore whatever misfortune they suffer at the hands of their former fellow Gaels is warranted: ". . . the Eireannaigh deserved that killing, for as the normannaigh do, so they also did."[26]

Cellacháin also distinguishes a group of Gaels who operate in Norse idiom but can be isolated from their actions by their parentage. In the twenty-third chapter, Cellachán and his men fight the amassed forces of the "inhabitants of Kerry [*Ciarrage*] and the Lochlannachs who previously had escaped from them in the Battle of Limerick." Cellachán succeeds and takes hostages of the combined forces, then is joined by Donnchuan mac Cennédig who:

> . . . began to inspect the Danair and the foreigners (*na neachtrainn*). At seeing him the [Gaelic] descendants of Eógan welcomed him and told him to remember his friendship. . . . Donnchuan assented to this, for he thought it was an evil thing to let the descendants of Eógan be slaughtered and reduced in numbers.[27]

*Echtrann** is translated by Bugge as "foreigners" and indeed has the connotation of one on a journey (*echtra*),[28] but this specific term exists in all of this dynastic propagandistic literature only in this precise setting, to describe Gaels of Munster allied with the Norse. Why else would the author distinguish the hostages under Donnchuan's purview as eachtrainn *alongside* the Danair? The term was utilized for the necessity to distinguish Norse allies, from the Norse themselves, as Gaels who had gone on a "journey" astray from the culture they were born into.

The reverse, inclusive terminology was also available in these Middle Irish texts for Norse operating in alliance with Gaels. The Battle of Clontarf involved Norse and Gaels on either side, even in the primary narrative given in the *Cogadh*, and was not a simple conflict between "native Gaels" and "foreign Norse" as portrayed in later nationalist material.† The Irish king Máel Mórdha and the men of Leinster famously opposed Brian's forces alongside Norse recruited from outside of Ireland. "As for Brian's forces in the battle, in fairness to the author of the *Cogadh* it must be said that he is very candid about the depleted nature of Brian's authority":

*In Irish, the grammatical morphology called *urú* or eclipsis sees a small consonant added to the following word which changes its initial sound.

†See, for instance, Brian Boru's supposed inclusion in the Irish independent political party Sinn Féin in a pamphlet on display at The Little Museum of Dublin.

the men of Munster, Connacht, and Mide (i.e., the forces of Máel Sechnaill II). *Cogadh* implies that Máel Sechnaill betrayed Brian by withdrawing from battle, whereas the *Annals of the Four Masters* ascribes the victory to his intervention after Brian's death.[29] There is an otherwise unnamed man in the Icelandic *Njáls Saga* who comes into the Icelanders' camp to broker a nonaggression pact, which can be explained as a reference to Máel Sechnaill agreeing to a secret truce with the Norse from outside of Ireland.

These men of Munster fighting for Brian must include those from the Hiberno-Norse towns Limerick, Waterford, and perhaps Cork and Wexford (see chapter 2), as described elsewhere in the *Cogadh*: "from all the men of Munster, Gall and Gael (*de feraib Muman uli eter gall ocus goedel*)."[30]

NORSE AND GAEL, AND NORSE-GAELIC MAGIC

The *Cogadh* also distinguishes the Norse from the Gael via idolatry, claiming in chapter sixty-nine that they were able to find and retrieve treasure throughout Ireland "through paganism and idol-worship (*tre geintilidhect ocus tre iodhaladhradh*)," though the specific mechanism is unmentioned. Notably, these Norse are written as able to penetrate "the various solitudes belonging to *Fianna* or to fairies (*ag Fianaibh no ag sithcuraibh*),"[31] which are clearly a native Gaelic tradition, outside of or at least ill at ease with the Christian church. The roughly contemporary twelfth-century Middle Irish text *Acallam na Senórach*, for instance, tells stories of the Fianna only within a larger frame narrative of St. Patrick expelling the warriors' demons, thus sanctifying their exploits for the written record: "*fianaigecht* ultimately accommodated within a Christian framework."[32]

The Norse "idolators," while coming from overseas, are not far removed from the Gaelic pre-Christian past; and Ireland, while Christian, still has places beyond control of the church, according to the author of these texts. This leakage of pre-Christian Ireland continues in *Cogadh*, where a supernatural host is seen in the sky before the aforementioned Battle of Clontarf:

> And there arose a wild . . . "vulture" (*badb*), screaming and fluttering over their heads.
>
> And there arose also the "satyrs" (*bananaig*), and the "idiots" (*boccanaig*) and the "maniacs of the valleys" (*geliti glini*), and the witches (*amati adgaill*) and "goblins" (*siabra*) . . . and they were screaming and comparing the valour and combat of both parties.[33]

Todd's 1857 translation includes colorful choices that obscure the Gaelic Irish origin of several of these supernatural creatures. "Badb" is better translated as a "hooded" or "scald-crow," but refers specifically to Morrígan, a goddess who takes the form of that bird.[34] *Bánánach* (variation of *bananaig*), *bocánach* (variation of *boccanaig*), and *genit* and "gelit glini" appear together in other twelfth century literature from the *Lebor na hUidre* and the Book of Leinster recension of the *Táin Bó Cuailnge*, with the former two repeated as well in contemporary fianaigecht material.[35]

As they appear to be stock characters of frenzy in Middle Irish literature, Todd's description of them with Latinate creatures of madness reflects a nineteenth-century preference for classical material that is not shared by the original. The siabra are another distinctly Gaelic Irish figure in the sky above the battle.[36] As these beings communicate with each other, and are talking about "both parties" in the conflict, this lends a supernatural milieu over all attendants present, whether Christian or, for the purposes of literary tension, heathen.

Brian exemplifies his sanctity by not engaging in the Battle of Clontarf at all. Instead, the admittedly quite old man prays for his troops in a tent nearby, and like Christ, he has foreseen his own death on Good Friday. Brian's death is foretold, however, by Aoibhell of Craglea (Aibhell Craicce Leithe),[37] "a supernatural lady who resided in the *síd* [burial mound] of Craig Liath, near Killaloe, co. Clare."[38] Brian also meets with, and directs the violent attentions of, the "supernatural being" Dúnlaing Ua hArtagáin during the conflict.[39]

This cast of non-Christian characters around Brian and his troops at Clontarf complicate the simple literary dichotomy of the righteous Gaelic Irish versus the evil heathen Norse. How can the Norse be accused of idolatry when Brian himself converses with supernatural creatures for his own benefit?

Before the Battle of Clontarf, Brian's career included the destruction of sacred inauguration sites of rival Gaelic kings, often marked by trees. The Dal gCáis themselves had a sacred tree at Mag Adair that was hewn by the king of Tara in 981, and apparently replanted only to be hewn again by the king of Connacht in 1051.[40] During the Battle of Clontarf, for dramatic effect, Brian's servant first compares the din of battle to the sound of Caill Tomair* being chopped down, and then later compares the battle to the sound of the same wood on fire.[41] Brian's destruction of the wood is part of his tactic to de-legitimize rival kings by literally uprooting their sources of inaugural power.

Not just the Norse are directly using magic, either. In the

*The "Wood of Þórr" in Dyflin, see chapter 1.

Cerball saga, the eponymous hero finds himself the victim of magic practiced by a fellow Gael:

> The learned (*na h-eolaigh*) related that Cerball had great difficulty there because Tairceltach mac na Cearta practiced magic upon him (*imirt draigheachta do . . . fair*) . . . [42]

The name Tairceltach only appears in Irish as a name of a learned man: there is a Taircelltach *sapiens* recorded in several Irish annals as well as a Taircelltach "next to the phrase *magica ars* in Berne Stadtbibliothek MS 363."[43] There is also the named father of a late ninth-century abbot of Clonmacnoise: "Blathmac son of Tairceltach (otherwise Taircedach), of Breghmaine, abbot."[44] The *Annals of Ulster* does not mention the father in their entry for Blathmac (896.1); but the *Annals of the Four Masters* 891.3 reads "*Blathmhac, mac Taircealtaigh, do Bregmainibh, abb Cluana Mic Nóis.*" This could also be a misspelling of the more common personal name Tairdealbach.

If "Taircel(l)tach" has mystical connotations—this Tairceltach's only appearance in *Cerball* is here, performing an enchantment—this may be the construction of a supernatural non-figure akin to the prior mentioned Dúnlaing Ua hArtagáin. "Na Cearta" means "the correct" or "righteous."[45] The twelfth-century *Lebor na gCert* is a Middle Irish text that "purports to record the rights of the Irish Kings, the King of Ireland, the provincial kings and the stipends due from the King of Ireland to the provincial kings."[46] Perhaps the second name ("mac" meaning "son [of]") indicates that this figure is an embodiment of the standard *cert* of kings, which Cerball here circumvents, and Tairceltach has been deputized to correct Cerball with magic.

Regardless, the name Tairceltach indicates that he is a Gael, not Norse. Therefore, just as Hona the Norse "druid" (*drui*) performs magic (*denamh a draoigheachta*)[47] against Cerball within the saga, so too can opponents who are clearly encoded with Gaelic names work against him with magic (imirt draigheachta).[48] For the Irish author of this text and their audience, the sort of enchantment available to magicians was the same for Norse and Gaelic practitioners.

CONCLUSIONS

These examples offer a tantalizing glimpse into the Middle Irish imagination of Norse heathen practice. The Gaels saw the Norse as "gentiles" and "idolators," but also recognized in these narratives that they had plenty in common with them: they saw both cultures praying to their deities before battle, utilizing sacred woods or trees, fairy or supernatural allies before and during warfare, church buildings as the site of religious ceremonies, and the use of enchantment or "druidry" to achieve magical ends.

The Norse were non-Christians, but so were the ancestors of the Gaels, and so for them Ireland was capable of hosting the heathen gods of Scandinavia through their followers, the Norse in Ireland. Such obvious references to "*draoichta*" on the part of Norse and Gaelic characters in these texts indicate that the authors, and their audience, did not see such things as impossibly ancient or locked away into exclusive ethnic capabilities, but as living and transitive traditions available to Norse, Gael, and Norse-Gael.

6
Folkways in the North Atlantic

"Útgarðaloki" in Context

The story of Þórr, Loki, and Þjalfi's visit to the fortress of Útgarðaloki is a distinctive and celebrated episode of the "Gylfaginning" section of the *Prose Edda*, an early thirteenth-century Icelandic text written by Snorri Sturluson. It is notable for its length, cohesive narrative, and connections with other Scandinavian texts under or outside Snorri's authorship. It also stands out as a humorous and self-contained story among many snippets of information about Norse mythology. Snorri did not include "Útgarðaloki" in "Gylfaginning" just because it is about two gods and a giant magician, but rather had a definite plan for the tale that involved creative synthesis, interest in the extra-Scandinavian folklore of former enslaved people in Iceland, and a desire to create "cultural capital" by his literary endeavors in Norway.

"Útgarðaloki" has elicited interest in its origins from essentially the beginning of modern Scandinavian literature studies, and scholarly opinion has yet to come down on one origin or another, including the concept that it "may be Snorri's own invention."[1] Recent genetic studies suggest that there were many more people of Gaelic (in this case, Irish and Scottish) descent, particularly women, involved in the settlement of Iceland. It is likely that this will push scholarly opinion into endorsing more firmly a Gaelic origin to the myth.

GAELIC MOTIFS IN ICELANDIC LITERATURE

The modern debate on the Gaelic-origin hypothesis began with Sophus Bugge's massive four-part work, *Studier over de nordiske Gude- og Heltesagns Oprindelse*, published in the 1880s.[2] A 1910 article by C. W. von Syndow entitled "Tors färd til Utgård" in *Danske Studier* continued Bugge's hypothesis; it was countered in 1921 in a section of Finnur Jónsson's *Norsk-islandske kultur-og sprogforhold i 9. og 10. årh.* The two scholars entered into a direct debate in 1922 with two articles in *Folkminnen och folktanker 8*.[3]

The most recent and definitive work explicitly about the Irish influence on "Útgarðaloki" is the 1985 article by Rosemary Power, "'An Óige, an Saol agus an Bas', *Feis Tighe Chonáin* and 'Þorr's Visit to Utgarða-Loki.'" "*An óige, an saol agus an bás*" literally means "youth, the world, and death" and it is an Irish folktale that exists in many different iterations. The common theme is that heroes journey to, or are led to, an unknown house with motley inhabitants such as a multicolored ram or sheep, a strong old man, an enticing young woman, and a fierce cat. The house inhabitants act oddly or say bizarre things to the guests, although they are treated well, and in the morning the residents' actions are explained as allegorical. Each version has a slightly different combination, but the most frequent allegories are that the ram or sheep is the World, the cat is Death, the old man is Old Age, and the young woman is Youth. While no single version is arrayed precisely as Snorri's "Útgarðaloki," the theme of travelers in a house of allegory is an obvious connection between the two stories, and the Irish Death-cat explains why the Midgarðsormur in Útgarðr is a cat, of all things.

Power does not stop there, however. She discusses other popular early Irish stories, including some that are dated to before the *Prose Edda*, such as the "Teach Cuana" episode of "Feast of the House of Conán" (*Feis Tighe Chonáin*) and "Cormac in the Land of Promise" (*Echtra Cormaic i Tir Tairngiri*), which also contain elements of otherworld visits and allegory. She builds a strong case for an Irish affinity for these motifs, making their singular appearance in Scandinavian literature almost certainly a sign of Irish influence in Iceland, or at the very least upon Snorri. Power writes, "It cannot therefore be assumed that the main tale was particularly well-known in Iceland, but it is unlikely that Snorri composed it himself or that he would have used it at all if he had not considered it to be traditional."[4]

1996 saw a more general reassessment of the Irish influence on Icelandic literature with the publication of Bo Almqvist's "Gaelic/Norse Folklore Contacts: Some Reflections on Their Scope and Character." In a thirty-three-page paper Almqvist spends one sentence on "Útgarðaloki," and that is to register his agreement with previous scholars on its Irish origins.[5]

USING GAELIC MATERIAL FOR GAIN

In *Snorri Sturluson and the* Edda*: The Conversion of Cultural Capital in Medieval Scandinavia*, Kevin J. Wanner argues that

Snorri composed the *Edda* in an attempt to make Iceland relevant to Norway despite the former's economic, populous, and historical comparative deficits. By making his quaint knowledge of skaldic poetry and pre-Christian mythology into a cohesive, comprehensive text, Snorri bought himself "cultural capital" in Norway that allowed him recognition and possibly financial gain. This is an interesting thesis that makes a novel conclusion out of frequently trodden information; Wanner acknowledges his debts to Anthony Faulkes, Sigurðal Nordal, Marlene Ciklamini, and other earlier scholars writing about Snorri and his motivations for composition. Wanner's main aim is "not so much to resolve the paradoxes that have surrounded the figure of Snorri as to dissolve them" by reconciling Snorri's social, political, and academic identities."[6]

What is really interesting, then, is why the strange story of Útgarðaloki is in the *Edda* at all. It does not appear anywhere else in Scandinavian early medieval literature, whereas almost everything else that Snorri writes turns up elsewhere in the corpus. Hilda Ellis Davidson writes, "the account of the contest in the giant's hall is witty and sophisticated, with use of allegory not normally found in Norse myths, but this does not mean that the framework of the tale was not based on an early source."[7] Snorri had a lot at stake in the composition and dissemination of his work, and the use of "Útgarðaloki" in his bid for relevancy indicates a confidence in the tale normally reserved for stories of obvious Scandinavian origin.

Importantly, "Útgarðaloki" fits. While the story itself has piqued interest due to its wit and sophistication, the context is well-integrated into the narrative that Snorri constructs. The story is introduced like every other section of "Gylfaginning," with a pointed question asked by Gylfi to the three lords of the hall, leading to a story in response. The lords seem hesitant to answer

Gylfi's question about whether Þórr has ever encountered anything magical that got the better of him, and attempt to dissuade him from asking it, but Gylfi persists; the story is narrated in several pages of speech. Nothing mentioned in the story directly contradicts the mythic worldview depicted elsewhere by Snorri or in other surviving skaldic poetry. However, there is some evidence of patchwork storytelling.

THE STORY OF ÚTGARÐALOKI

Within the story, Þórr travels eastward to the land of the giants just as he does in other texts outside of Snorri's work: Þórr "began [his] journey east into Giant-land (*byrjaði ferðina austr í Jötunheima*)." The prose introduction to "Lokasenna" in the *Codex Regius* mentions that "Þórr came not, because he was in [the] east (*Þórr kom eigi, þvíat hann var í austrvegi*)." Þórr also mentions several occasions where he went east to fight giants in "Hárbarðzlióð," and like in "Lokasenna," it is brought up against him that he hid in a glove. In the former, Loki says, "since in a glove thumb you sat cowering, warrior / and seemed not to be Þórr then (*sízt í hansca þumlungi hnúcþir þú einheri / oc þóttisca þú þá Þórr vera*)," while in the latter Harbarð proclaims, "from cowardice and fear you were crammed in a glove / and seemed not to be Þórr then (*af hræzlo oc hugbleyði þér var in hanzca troðit, / oc þóttisca þú þá Þórr vera*)."

Clearly there is some sort of overlap between these poems in the word-for-word repetition, which occurs at the end of stanza 60 in "Lokasenna" and in the second line of a four- line stanza, 26, in "Hárbarðzlióð." What is interesting, though, is where each poem goes from there. Loki also taunts Þórr about the trip to Útgarðaloki by mentioning Skrymir's *scarpar álar* (hardened leather straps) that

Þórr could not undo, which fits in well with Snorri's "Útgarðaloki." However, Power explains that "[a]lthough these stanzas both refer to incidents on the journey [to Útgarðaloki] it is not clear whether they were even included in the same tale at this stage, as the stanzas are separated from each other by one which contains a reference to the quite different tale of Þórr's slaying of Hrungnir."[9]

"Hárbarðzlióð," on the other hand, tells of a different story where Þórr hides in a glove- thumb from a giant Fiallar and was "guarding a river, / when Svárang's sons sought me" (*ána varðac, / þá er mic sótto þeir Svárangs synir*). The conversation between Harbarð and Þórr typically involves questioning what the other was doing when one was being courageous; Harbarð turns this on Þórr in relation to the glove incident, and then Þórr talks about fighting the sons of Svárang in his defense. This is even better evidence that there was a motif in Icelandic storytelling about Þórr in a glove-thumb that existed outside of Snorri's "Útgarðaloki."

We are thus possibly witnessing a seam in Snorri's work. The only Fiallar in the *Prose*

Edda is the murderous dwarf Fjalar from the "Skáldskaparmál," and the only name somewhat similar to Svárang is another dwarf, Svarin, from whose grave mound many dwarves are recorded as coming from in "Gylfaginning." It would possibly make sense to have a murderous dwarf going after Þórr, and an ensuing fight with that dwarf and others described as a battle with "Svarin's sons." However, it is inherently difficult to rectify how Þórr would end up in a massive glove's thumb if he was fighting with dwarves. Whether the Fiallar of "Hárbarðzlióð" and the Fjalar of the *Prose Edda* are related or not, there is something strange in the subtle discrepancies between the texts. It may be that Snorri knew that there was some story involving Þórr in a glove, based on a kenning, and inserted this scene into "Útgarðaloki." If so, it attests to his creativity, because it fits within the narrative well.

It also accords with the "flow" of "Gylfaginning," as well as a framing story of a traveler asking very specific questions of three noble strangers can have a narrative. The episode immediately following "Útgarðaloki" is sequential within the *Prose Edda* as well as corroborative with other Icelandic literature. After his encounter with the cat Midgarðsormur, Þórr goes to test his strength against the undisguised monster, just as "Völuspá" says he will do at Ragnarök.

Finally, and very importantly, "Útgarðaloki" is a significant portion of "Gylfaginning." It is the longest unbroken narrative by many words; the only other long section is the much more mythologically consequential tale of Baldr's death. The lord Þriði characterizes "Útgarðloki" as "tidings that are not able to be said by us as fine" (*tíðindi vita þótt oss þykki eigi fagrt at segja*) while the lord Hár describes the tale of Baldr's death as "tidings [that] are thought more significant to [the] Æsir" (*tíðindum er meira þótti vert Ásunum*). As Baldr's death is told immediately after the episode of Þórr's intentional encounter with the Midgarðsormur, it can be presumed that the comparative meira refers back to this, and possibly therefore back to "Útgarðaloki."

WRITING MYTHOLOGICAL MATERIAL

As a trained Christian cleric, Snorri is probably not speaking through his narrators about the importance of one mythic story over another. But as an author, however, the preference of a tale can be seen in the prominence that "Útgarðaloki" enjoys just by the amount of vellum required to record every detail.

Therefore, between its cohesion with the corpus of Scandinavian literature, possibly with some alteration to incorporate elements from unrelated stories, its narrative fit within the *Prose Edda*, and simply the large amount of space that it occupies, it is obvious that Snorri meant for "Útgarðaloki" to be a significant part of his important work. His motivation is not so clear, however. It appears according to surviving records that it was a story known only in Iceland and Snorri may have felt the need to describe it in detail, as opposed to creation myths or stories about the Æsir that his Norwegian benefactors would already be acquainted with. It may have been a story intentionally given prominence based on its content, or its origin. It could have also intentionally been a pastiche intended to demonstrate Snorri's originality in the midst of what was essentially an anthology or catalog of preexisting tales, or a combination of any or all of these.

Wanner's theory of cultural capital claims that Iceland's main export during the Sturlung Age that Snorri occupied (and helped to define) was the production of poetry. Clever, well- versed skalds producing strong literature were therefore able to win kings and influence patrons despite their nation's impoverishment. Wanner explains that "The Edda . . . was Snorri's attempt, in the face of forces and circumstances that threatened the value of his cultural resources, to preserve and, if possible, reinvigorate the capacity of skaldic verse to act as capital within Scandinavian circles of power."[11]

The "Háttatal" portion of the *Prose Edda* is a praise poem written for two specific men,

King Håkon and Duke Skúli. The other two sections are intended as a manual for composing poetry in the traditional manner, in the face of the newer, more fashionable verse forms of continental Europe. The composition of "Gylfaginning" and

"Skáldskaparmál" were not Snorri putting on a show of being quaint for his Norwegian patrons or compiling mythology for fun; he had the much more serious mission of maintaining his relevancy outside of Iceland. He may also have been struggling to maintain Icelanders' identity in the face of several powerful Norwegian kings who could have considered Iceland to be a cultural backwater, or an extension of Norway that needed to be part of the kingdom, or both.

The twelfth-century Icelandic settlement history *Landnámabók* demonstrates cultural anxiety about the legitimacy of Icelanders in the early medieval period. The epilogue from the Þórðarbók version includes, "It is often said that writing about the settlements is irrelevant learning, but we think we can all the better meet the criticisms of foreigners when they accuse us of being descended from slaves or scoundrels, if we know for certain the truth about our ancestry."[12] Characters in the sagas of Icelanders are often described as noble and the authors go to great lengths to describe their honorable ancestry. The reason for this anxiety was revealed in Agnar Helgason and colleagues' genetic discovery that a significant proportion of Icelanders at settlement, and a majority of women, were from Ireland and Scotland; most against their will as captured slaves.[13]

CONCLUSIONS

Like the Midgarðsormur, here we find ourselves catching a glimpse of our own tail. Medieval Icelanders were more or less conscious of the Gaelic heritage inherently interwoven into their society by the inclusion of so many Gaels at settlement. The subsequent absorption of the slave class resulted in a syncretism of Gaelic and Norse to create a medieval Icelandic identity, where Old Norse is metaphorically and figuratively the language of the people, but Middle Irish concepts live on outside of their natural habitat. If we follow the prevailing theory of an Irish origin for all or most of "Útgarðaloki," we then arrive at a story brought to Iceland by enslaved people, utilized by a thirteenth-century Icelander of some social importance, in a bid for continued acceptance of traditional verse forms by Norwegians of rank and power. These are quite long legs for what is usually considered a take-it-or-leave-it piece of Eddaic folklore!

Why, then, did Snorri choose this particular story of extra-Scandinavian origin to take up so much of his manual of mythology? Other tales in other places demonstrate Irish influence, such as the similarities between Loki in *Lokasenna* and Bricriu in the eighth century "The Feast of Bricriu" (*Fled Bricrenn*),[14] and the appearance of an Irish *each-uisge* (water-horse) in *Landnámabók*.[15]

Snorri probably had no shortage of folktales that would be novel to his Norwegian audience. The tale of a journey to the east, to be ridiculed by powerful giants who turn out to be illusions, seems to be an impudent gift for powerful patrons in Norway who are, after all, an eastward journey from Iceland. It is also quite unlike most of the rest of skaldic poetry which seeks to heap praise on the recipient, usually in reference to his or her hospitality and generosity, as Útgarðaloki begins as a wretched host.

In fact, this is opposite from Irish tales of this type where the Otherworldly host treats his guests well. As Power points out,

> The manner in which Útgarðaloki suddenly becomes amicable and freely volunteers the explanations to the humiliated Þórr provides another link with the Irish tales, and . . . suggests that the host was not originally an enemy of the companions, and therefore that this tale did not originally concern Þórr and the giants. . . . It is understandable that the giants should wish to play a trick

> on Þórr, but it is odd that Útgarðaloki should praise the companions' prowess and admit how afraid the giants were. . . .[16]

Instead of a content-specific reason to feature "Útgarðaloki," I personally think that Snorri intended to demonstrate his creative potential while cleaning up loose ends from kennings and unknown references from poetry.

The most obvious mark of Snorri's originality is that "Útgarðaloki" is a microcosm of "Gylfaginning." Both Gylfi and Þórr travel to distant lands and meet strange and powerful foreigners in a hall or fortress that disappears after the events of the visit have played out. This in itself may be an Irish motif: "Gylfi and his adventures are not known in any older Norse sources, and it was possible that this frame tale was constructed by Snorri himself."[17] If Snorri created the "Gylfaginning" frame tale to organize disparate kennings and mythological trivia into something of a narrative, it is very possible that he also soldered some poetic odds and ends into "Útgarðaloki."

This would also help to explain its place in "Gylfaginning" rather than in "Skáldskaparmál." The former is mostly facts and anecdotes about the gods and other Norse cosmological elements while the latter is mostly longer episodes that explain kennings. Snorri does not make any explicit kennings out of "Útgarðaloki" in "Gylfaginning," but "Skáldskaparmál" includes a kenning for Þórr as "the lord of Þjálfi and Röskva" (*dróttinn Þjálfa ok Rösku*). There is a hint in "Hárbarðzlióð" and a few lines in "Skáldskaparmál" that identify Þjálfi as a helpful servant of Þórr, particularly in connection with the latter's slaying of the giant Hrungnir, but Röskva appears nowhere else in the surviving literature.

It would seem then that this story, which offers nothing new about gods or cosmological concepts, would belong in the section where Snorri goes to great lengths to explain kennings with a series of unrelated stories. However, if he had managed to fit disparate elements of Scandinavian poetry into a workable and amusing tale, he would probably consider it just as important to his readers as, for example, the origins of the sun and moon.

Thus the composition of Snorri's "Útgarðaloki" and its inclusion in "Gylfaginning" had several distinct intentions that were separate but not at cross purposes. The first was simply to add more material to his guide to the Norse cosmology for Scandinavian poets, like himself, who were facing extinction due to the popularity of imported continental literature and verse forms. The second was to tie together several unrelated elements referenced in earlier poetry into a cohesive pastiche. The third was to make use of motifs of Irish folklore that had become a part of Icelandic storytelling with the subsuming of the enslaved class since settlement, which would be novel to Norwegians. Altogether, Snorri was looking to show off his skills in secular scholarship and skaldic poetry as well as keep his skills in demand overseas. "Útgarðaloki" is a product of a brilliant medieval mind looking out for its own best interests.

7
Norse-Gaelic Paganism in Practice

The previous chapters have shown us what, when, where, and how Norse-Gaelic paganism was practiced in the ninth to twelfth centuries and, in lesser forms, beyond. Hopefully, you the reader are now asking *why* should this culture be revived and celebrated today. *How* can we do so usefully, respectfully, and practically? *What* does it look and sound like, and *who* can become a Norse-Gaelic pagan?

The last question is easiest to answer. **Norse-Gaelic paganism is for absolutely anyone who feels the pull toward it *and* does the work to understand it.** We are the culture we inhabit. If you or your believed ancestors happen to be from the areas in which the Norse-Gaels operated, and this makes you feel like it is especially important for you, then by all means practice it. But do not mistake modern ideas of genealogy and genetics for the medieval concept of *gens*, contemporary with the Norse-Gaels and thus familiar to their worldview, even if they were not philosophers who used the term explicitly. Gens posits that one's family and descent were due to performance and mutable, rather than inherent and unchangeable.* The Gall-Gaedil with which this book begins are a prime example of this phenomenon: "Gaels" by birth have become "Foreigners" by their actions.

The Norse-Gaelic gods and ancestors do not care about the color of your skin or hair, your last name, your physical capabilities or gender or any of these things. Rather, they are there for those of us who strive to be like them, to learn their languages and think about seeing the world in the ways that they did (the whole world, that is, not just the North Atlantic). When we seek out the arts and literatures of the Norse-Gaels with our hearts and minds, we shine light on a dimmed world, and with enough practice and time, we can walk there without a torch in hand.

THE NORSE-GAELIC GODS

As a nonhierarchical religion—indeed, pushing the limits of the very term "religion"—Norse-Gaelic paganism did not have a centralized priesthood or organized dogmatic beliefs to standardize practice. There was not an established list of gods, but neither were there formal pantheons of either the Gaelic or Norse pre-Christian deities until later medieval writers attempted to categorize them. It was ad hoc at all times and places, but this transient quality makes Norse-Gaelic paganism more accessible to us in the present.

As established by the preceding chapters, the worship of local sites and veneration of ancestors were paramount. But the gods were present, and their roles and functions probably differed from household to household, or even practitioner to practitioner. The

*The best recent work on *gens* and medieval identification structure is Heng's *The Invention of Race in the European Middle Ages*, particularly the first chapter.

Icelandic family sagas recorded people who were dedicated to a single deity (henotheist, believing in multiple gods, but devoted to one of them alone) and people who were uninterested in the gods entirely (atheist, or perhaps agnostic in modern parlance).

Clearly, the survival of many names of Gaelic and Norse gods in medieval literature indicates that the end of a polytheistic worldview in the early medieval period did not instantly extinguish or eradicate these deities. The Norse-Gaels themselves occupied a world that was under political pressure to convert and remain Christian, and churches and monasteries were critical places of secular power. Nonetheless, the old gods persisted. A singular list of Norse-Gaelic gods would always be both deficient and misleading, because they were never organized into a Roman-style pantheon with a clear-cut set of relationships and obligations. But we know stories were told about them, from what was recorded in Iceland and Ireland, and over the years the Kindred of Mann has found the following deities most compelling for modern practitioners.

Brigit (BREE-/x/it)*: Modern English "Bridget," Modern Irish "Bríd," Scottish Gaelic "Brìghde," Manx "Breeshey." This well-beloved goddess-*cum*-saint is celebrated today by both Catholics and Irish-focused pagans worldwide, and she had a similar reach in medieval times. The Swedish queen Birgitta (d. 1208) was named for a family member who had originally come from Ireland, bringing this name into popularity in Scandinavia, and the medieval Christian descendants of the Norse-Gaels set up churches for the Irish saint Brigid outside of Ireland.

*All pronunciations are approximate, and intended as a starting point rather than the final pronouncement. The International Phonetic Alphabet symbol /x/ is a voiceless velar fricative, that is, a back-of-the-throat sound not found in modern English.

According to *Sanas Cormaic* she is a deity (or perhaps three) of poetry, blacksmithing, midwifery, and healing. Because of this she endows Norse-Gaelic paganism as a goddess of intuition, medicine, creativity, and protection.

Frígan** (*FREE-gon*): The presence of the völva's staff in Dyflin (see chapter 1), along with the literary evidence of seiðr in Clonmacnoise (see chapter 2), indicates that female-centered magic in a Norse idiom was practiced in Ireland. Icelandic sources attribute magical knowledge to the worship of both Freyja and her *valkyrja*, and Frigga and her handmaidens; they also imply that they are an exclusively feminine practice unsuitable for masculine practitioners or male gods. Unfortunately we do not have the name of any Norse goddesses in the medieval Irish language. I have impertinently combined the name Frigga and the word for "queen" in Old Irish, ***rígain, into a modern name for a medieval concept: **Frígan*, the Norse-Gael deity of feminine mysticism.

Loki (LOH-kee): This god appears throughout the Icelandic *Edda* material as a goading inciter and trickster figure, but also a traveling companion of Þórr and ancient friend of Óðinn. He is also the hero of the Faroese ballad "Loka Tattur," as well as the possible namesake of Lokkafelli, a mountain in Eysturøy in the Faroe Islands. While many modern heathens see Loki as a problematic, even hateful figure, the god's frequent appearance in North Atlantic material indicates that for Norse-Gaelic pagans, he was an important aspect of their cosmology. Kindred of Mann has always celebrated Loki as an integral part of our worldview.

Lugh (LOO/x/): Modern Irish "Lú." (Note that "lugh" is Manx for "mouse"!) Beloved of the fianna and the mythical father of Irish heroes, Lugh is a deity of poetry, dexterity, and craft, and is celebrated today as a polymath and master-of-all-trades. Among his epithets are *Samildánach*, "equally skilled in all the arts," and in surviving myths he serves as an itinerant craftsman and warrior who challenges established hierarchies and becomes king. Etymologically speaking, it is possible that Lugh and Loki share a prehistoric root in their names, but for the Norse-Gaels these would have been two very different gods.

Mannanán (MON-oh-nawn): The patron god of our kindred and the Isle of Man, Mannanán is euhemerized in *Sanas Cormaic* as a merchant who had power over storms. Traditionally, the triple legs on the Manx flag are the form he took to roll down and prevent the legendary Saint Patrick from landing on Mann! Manannán, however, is an epithet meaning "Manxman" as in *from* the Isle of Man; his proper name is actually Orbsen MacAlloid (ORV-shin moc-AHLL-uth). Lough Corrib outside Galway City is a corruption of *Lough Orrib*, "Orbsen's Lake." From his medieval literary roles as a sailor, trader, and islander, Manannán is celebrated today as both a literal seafarer as well as a god of transit, weather, and literal and metaphorical journeys.

Morrígan (*MOR-ee-gon*): An Irish goddess who also incorporates the title *rígan*, "queen." While the first element of her name is sometimes interpreted as *mór*, "great," even in later medieval texts, it is actually better translated as *mor*, "horror, phantom, destructive spirit," cognate with the "mare" of English "nightmare." The fíanna and *díberga*, who lived in the woods of Ireland outside of social norms, were associated with her, particularly in the form of badb, the hooded crow.[1] As the fíanna were interrelated with the *Gall Gaidheal*, and Morrígan is a goddess of warfare and people outside of society, she is a valued deity of the Norse-Gaelic worldview.

Odund (*OH-thin*): Modern English "Odin," Old Icelandic "Óðinn." Appearing among participants in the invasion of Ireland, a "fleet of Odund" (*longes Oduind*) has been translated as the possessive form of the Old Norse personal name *Auðunn* for centuries.[2] But with fictional and indeed semi-mythical companions in this ship-flood, I argue that this is more likely the Irish language rendition of the Norse god and his arrival in Ireland. The titular character of "Rígsþula," a fourteenth-century Eddic poem that has survived in one copy, may be another name for Odund,[3] as *rí(g)* is Middle Irish for "king." How else would this isolated Irish title appear in an Icelandic-language manuscript if not packaged with the god himself as a Norse-Gaelic rí? Odund is a god of madness, masculine and queer magic, inspiration, and cunning. With his role in the Útgarðaloki story and prominence elsewhere in the Icelandic material, Odund was clearly compelling to the Norse-Gaels.

Tomhar (TO-ver; variant forms include Tomar, Tomair, Tomhar, and Tomhair): Modern English "Thor," Old Icelandic "Þórr." Demonstrably the most characteristic god of the Norse in Ireland, in the form of Caill Tomhair (see chapter 1), and their appellation as "the family/people of Tomhar (muintir Tomhair)" in the *Cogadh*. Tomhar in the form of "Þórr" was also very important to the people of early Iceland, at least for the sheer number of "Þór-" personal names in the sagas.

NORSE-GAELIC HOLIDAYS

Modern pagans are well-acquainted with an eight-holiday annual system termed "The Wheel of the Year," with celebrations spread evenly about every six weeks apart. Different traditions uphold different holidays as most important: for example, Norse heathens generally see Yule and Midsummer as the "big ones," whereas Irish-focused pagans plan their years around Bealtaine and Samhain. Different traditions have different parameters as well for when the holidays are celebrated, such as if their date is also calculated by a lunar calendar or affected by observation in nature. Pragmatically, however, nearly all of today's pagans and heathens set their feast days by available weekends and the logistics of time off!

While the Wheel of the Year has brought a lot of joy to modern pagans, particularly converts and parents who want the regular rhythm of celebrating every month and a half, it is very much a modern construction only appropriate for a post-farming economy. Simply put, without refrigeration and reliable long-distance food transport, a year naturally sees both plenty and hunger in it, and the pre-modern calendar included feast periods as well as ebbs. It would have been foolish to gather and celebrate equally throughout the year. If the Wheel of the Year brings you satisfaction, of course, continue to celebrate it; but if you are looking for an annual cycle in the Norse-Gaelic tradition, there are clusters of holidays and then fallow periods for personal reflection.

Kindred of Mann began celebrating holidays in 2009, and over the years, six main feast-days have emerged, as a "summer" and "winter" matched set. If there is an axis for our holidays, it would be through the February and the August celebrations for Brigit and Lugh. These correspond to the height-and-descent of the warmest and coldest months of the year respectively in the Northern Hemisphere. Practically, it means celebrating toward the end of the American summer season and in the lull after secular New Year's Day, which brings a bit of excitement in to otherwise undistinguished periods of the year. These are holidays that have worked for us over time as annual celebrations, but it is not meant as a definitive calendar.

Boaldyn/Bealtaine: The first of the summer holidays, celebrated around the first of May in the familiar Gregorian calendar. The modern Irish name for month of May is Bealtaine (BYEL-taw-nuh) and it is considered the first day of summer. This is a holiday that was ancient before the Norse-Gaels ever came into being,[4] and while the origin of the name is debated, it is likely that the medieval mind envisioned the etymology of Bealtaine as coming from something like *Bél-Teine*, "Mouth-Fire." In the ninth through twelfth centuries, this holiday was likely seen as a celebration of the end of the winter, a return to primarily outdoor living, and enough fresh food to support spending time together.

Midsummer: The height of summer, and in the northern latitudes of the North Atlantic, a time of the longest days and little darkness at night. Midsummer is still celebrated in many Scandinavian communities there and abroad as the most cheerful, and perhaps a bit sleep-deprived, time of the year. On the Isle of Man, this is also the time for the Tynwald (*Laa Tinvaal*), the all-island legislature's ceremonial meeting out of doors. This is the day that Manannán receives his "rent" of rushes and meadow grasses, given at either the seaside itself or at the nearest river to the ocean.

Laa Luanys/Aonach/Þing: In Irish mythology, August was the time for festivals, fairs, and competitions (*oenach* in Old Irish, *aonach* in modern). The god Lú is still remembered in the modern Irish for the month of August, Lúnasa, and the Manx term for this holiday is Laa Luanys, Day of Lugh. For the Kindred of Mann this month is also for the regional heathen gathering now called Northeast Thing. The Norse *þing* (from which comes Manx *Tinvaal*, Icelandic *Alþing*, Norwegian *Gulating*, and others) was a combination legal and social meeting to address disputes, sell goods, see far-flung friends and relations, play games, and otherwise come together across a great distance annually. Northeast Thing brings heathens from as far as Virginia, Ohio, and Maine (and beyond!) to northeastern Pennsylvania for five days of both silly fun and holy solemnity.

Sauin/Hop-tu-Naa/Samhain: The dark half of the year begins with the celebration for the dead that partially inspired the modern Halloween. On the Isle of Man, October 31st is the night before Sauin (*Oie Houney*, Irish *Oíche Shamhna*) as well as the community-centered *Hop-tu-Naa*. While carved turnips are involved—often cited as a pre-cursor to the New World pumpkins made into jack o'lanterns—turnips are not native to the Isle of Man. This festival is more about fun, family, and remembering the ancestors as a community.

Yule/Midwinter: This holiday appears in Old Norse material as an important feast for both host and attendees, but its exact timing is unknown; modern heathens tend to pin it to the December solstice around the 21st. Yule tends to get conflated with Christmas, for better or worse; some practitioners like having a reason to celebrate alongside their Christian friends, coworkers, and family members; others prefer keeping their traditions distinct from the socially dominant holiday.

Laa'l Breeshey/Þorrablót/Up Helly Aa: The end of January and beginning of February sees a bounty of holidays from around the North Atlantic that Kindred of Mann has blended together into a special celebration that enlivens what is often the greyest and coldest part of the year. Laa'l Breeshey is the Manx name for Irish Lá Féile Brigte or the Feast-day of Brigit, also known from the sources as Imbolc (IMMb-ol-ig). This is traditionally when lambs arrived and ewes began lactating, bringing fresh dairy into an otherwise dried out winter diet. In Ireland, rushes and straw are plaited together into crosses and the *críos Brídhe* (literally "girdle," but an archway to walk through for blessing). "Þorrablót" comes from earlier modern Iceland and is *not* a celebration for Þórr but rather Þorri, a winter frost-giant. It is a national holiday that centers on the more unusual and distinctive of Icelandic dishes such as *hákarl*, due to their appearance on the dinner table at this leanest time of year. Kindred of Mann celebrates Þorrablót with atypical foods and silly hats. Finally, various places in the Shetland Islands burn replica Viking ships at the end of January.

LANGUAGE AND LITURGY

Of course, the gods understand modern English and its idioms; they hear the cries of the heart, not the pattern of the syllables in which they are called. However, striving to speak to them in Middle Irish or Old Norse, or languages descended from them such as Manx and Icelandic, helps us learn how to shape our minds in ways that would have been more familiar to the Norse-Gaels.

Presuming you, the reader, are an English speaker, you are already comfortable with a language that has no proper future tense. It is a common characteristic of Germanic languages (which include Old Norse and English) to require helping verbs and other indicators to imply action in the future. We tend not to think about it outside of a language class because we're trained from the start to add "will" to a phrase to make it happen in the future: I go (now), I will go (later). This is a rather peculiar way of seeing the world, where we can only plan for the future, but things that are happening or have happened are concrete and established.

Old and Middle Irish and its descendants, modern Irish, Scottish Gaelic,* and Manx, also bear a panoply of fascinating linguistic principles that are unfamiliar to most English speakers. Initial mutations seem maddening, where leniting h's and lowercase eclipsing letters seem to come out of nowhere in Irish and Gaelic. Perhaps even more confusingly, the beginning letter of words can change in Manx. Concepts like the consuetudinal present, emphatics, reflexives, and ubiquitous verbal nouns convey ideas that are difficult to express in English. These indicate a way of thinking about the world and performing actions that are different from a Germanic-framed style of thinking.

If you are as unlikely to teach yourself Irish as you are to grow wings, however, you can also get a feel for some of these idiosyncrasies by reading or listening to Hiberno-English literature. Aspects of the Irish language have filtered into how English is spoken in Ireland, even among people who don't speak Irish. For instance, there is no single word to express "yes" or "no" in Irish, so to agree or disagree with a statement or question, the respondent repeats the verb in the positive or negative. In Hiberno-English, this appears as a reluctance to answer questions directly but to emphasize the response with a repetition of the verb. For instance:

"DID YOU GO TO THE CINEMA?"

"I DID, YEAH."

*Also called simply Gaelic, or archaically, Scots-Gaelic. This is *not* the language called Scots, which is in the Germanic family and closely related to English.

"Have you a Euro?"

"I haven't, no."

The works of James Joyce are a treasure trove of Hiberno-English, though it is also readily available in more accessible writing by authors like Edna O'Brien and Colm Toibín. Hearing these works read aloud via audiobooks may help if they are difficult to understand in print.

As readers can probably guess, I am a proponent of using the languages of the Norse-Gaels in private devotion and communal worship—*insofar as the participants can understand it.* The last thing I want to advocate for is prayer that requires phonetic memorization, or a ceremony spent standing around feeling silly while an officiant drones on in a foreign language! Rather, the use of (and instruction in) a small amount of Middle Irish and/or Old Norse helps to contexualize the sources that are called upon to inform the practice.

Critically, the Norse-Gaels would have *themselves* navigated the waters of thinking and feeling in different languages. It is fascinating to imagine how a native Norse speaker would have explained their philosophy to a native Irish speaker and vice versa in the pidgin that they would use to communicate with one another until they shared a common language.

That said, it is more important to reach people's hearts than their minds, and for that reason the main devotional liturgy of ritual deposition in the Kindred of Mann is in plain modern English. I encourage readers whose everyday vernacular is *not* English to translate this into familiar language, for their own benefit and for the good of any other attendees. It is far more important to do the thing than to not do it, in fear of not doing it properly.

(This is, incidentally, the driving force of this entire book.)

The following lines are spoken aloud by all when the food, drink, or other offerings hallowed by the ceremony are being buried (or, in the case of inclement weather or frozen ground, placed outside of the dwelling space to be deposited later):

From the earth we've come*
To the earth we'll go
From us above
To the gods below.
Hail! Sláinte!

Depending on the gods of the occasion is whether we use "hail" (a modern English version of a pan-Germanic cheer) or "sláinte" (Irish), both meaning "health" and its larger ideas of haleness and wholeness.

The two primary offering types are the blót, the original of which is referenced several times in the Icelandic material, and the *idbart* ("ITH-verd"), which is a modern reconstruction of the Old Irish word for sacrifice, and unrelated to Latinate terms that came in with Christianity. As modern heathens, our blót offering material is typically homemade (or rather, friend-made) mead, but we also use nonalcoholic drinks as the situation requires. While drinking horns are a part of Old Norse culture via the literature and archeology, they were drinking vessels like any other, and it is very much a contemporary affectation to use them in ritual.

Had the pre-Christian religion(s) of northern Europe continued

*"Earth" in the sense of soil, rather than the literal planet.

without disruption, surely this mode of communal drinking would have adapted with changing fashions in drinkware, and there would be nothing special about the early medieval period or its objects. But as heathens today, we are intentionally retroactive (perhaps even retro-activists!). We are the other side of a bridge that soars over hundreds of years. While there's nothing particularly holy or heathen about medieval garments or reconstructed language, if it brings participants into a mindset where they feel better able to reach across the span of time to the last of the prior blót-makers with the name of our gods in their mouths, then we should not scoff at or eschew this bit of theatricality.

Similarly, the idbart is the generic idea of a blót but in a Gaelic idiom. Food is made to be eaten in a shared setting as we speak our hopes, fears, thanks, and other messages for the gods and ancestors. These words permeate the food and then we bury it out of sight. Early worries about being called an ahistorical fusion led Kindred of Mann to carefully distinguish sacrifices to Norse and Irish gods, but over time and reflecting on the relative successes and satisfactions of ritual, it has become more a distinction between living drink (i.e., the products of fermentation) and food that was once alive, whether plant, fungi, or animal. In both cases, however, the altered substances go under the ground, or under water if a large enough body is available, to be unseen and hidden, and thus transmuted to the world that is Other, where the gods and ancestors dwell.

CONCLUSION

What lies before us? Far be it from me to imply that this book is an instruction manual or a prescription for thoughts or behavior. Rather, I have laid out some canals and engineered water dispensation in an arid landscape, the valley between modern Norse heathenism and Celtic reconstructionism. I hope that you, the reader, will go and see what sort of wildflowers are in bloom there.

Notes

INTRODUCTION

1. Radner, *Fragmentary Annals*, 105.
2. Downham, "The Good, the Bad and the Ugly," 32–33.
3. Moore, *Folk-Lore*, 147.
4. Ó Cróinín, *New History of Ireland*, 212–13.
5. Bibire, "North Sea Language," 88–89.
6. Kunz, "Saga of the People," 276.
7. Terry, *Poems*, xvii.

1. DYFLIN

1. Simpson, "Viking Warrior Burials", 16.
2. Holm, "Naval Power," 74.
3. Ó Cróinín, *Early Medieval*, 260.
4. Duffy, "Reconsideration," 358.
5. Marstrander, *Bidreg*, 66, 109, 127.
6. Todd, *Cogadh*, 30–31.
7. Duffy, *Brian Boru*, 214–15.
8. Duffy, *Brian Boru*, 201.
9. Price, *Viking Way*, 159–60.

10. Wallace, "Meagre Lead," 271–72.
11. Clarke et al., *Dublin and the Viking World*, 100.

2. ELSEWHERE IN IRELAND

1. Hughes et al., *Place-Names of Northern Ireland*, vol. 2, 7.
2. Todd, *Cogadh*, 81.
3. Todd, *Cogadh*, 79.
4. Todd, *Cogadh*, 85.
5. Bugge, *Cellacháin*, 66.
6. Radner, *Fragmentary Annals*, 109.
7. Radner, *Fragmentary Annals*, 125.
8. Bugge, *Cellacháin*, 70–71.
9. Bugge, *Cellacháin*, 33.
10. Allan, "Poet," 16.
11. Allan, "Poet," 14.
12. eDIL, s.v. *geis*.
13. Todd, *Cogadh*, 12.
14. Lunde and Stone, *Ibn Fadlān*, 52.
15. Frank, "Boar on the Helmet" and "*Beowulf* and Sutton Hoo."
16. Suppe, "'Irish' Welshmen." See also Wadden, "Theories."
17. Foster, *Oxford Illustrated History*, 33.
18. Downham, "The Good, the Bad and the Ugly."
19. Hudson, "Lothlind."

3. THE NORTHERN AND SOUTHERN ISLES

1. R. A. McDonald, *Sea Kings*, chapter 3
2. Dumville, "Old Dubliners," 81.
3. Bugge, *Chellacháin*, 24.
4. Hermann and Edwards, *Landnámabók*, 32.
5. Etchingham et al., *Norse-Gaelic Contacts*, 302.

6. Hermann and Edwards, *Landnámabók,* 32.
7. Etchingham, et al., *Norse-Gaelic Contacts*, 300.
8. Hermann and Edwards, *Landnámabók,* 42–43.
9. Hermann and Edwards, *Landnámabók,* 83, 88.
10. Hermann and Edwards, *Landnámabók,* 95.
11. Kunz, "Saga of the People," 285.
12. Etchingham et al., *Norse-Gaelic Contacts*, 363.
13. Clunies Ross, *Poetry*, 842.
14. Kunz, "Saga of the People," 333.
15. MacNiven, *Vikings*, 113.
16. R. A. McDonald, "Man, Ireland, and England," 132, fn. 7.
17. Steinforth, "Early Vikings," passim.
18. Duffy, "Irishmen and Islesmen," passim.

4. GAELS IN THE SETTLEMENT OF ICELAND

1. Agnar et al., "Estimating" and Agnar et al., "mtDNA."
2. Hermann and Edwards, *Landnámabók*, 147 (with several personal emendments noted in underline).
3. Jón Jóhannesson, *History*, 118.
4. Turville-Petre, "Cult of Óðinn," 4.
5. Lyall, "Building."
6. Lenihan and Green, *Meeting*, 121–23,
7. Snorri, *Prose Edda*, 25–26.
8. Dooley and Roe, *Tales of the Elders*, 5, 12.
9. Gantz, *Early Irish Myths and Sagas* (both stories).
10. Turville-Petre, "Cult of Óðinn," 6.
11. Hermann and Edwards, *Landnámabók*, 19–20.
12. Hermann and Edwards, *Landnámabók*, 22.
13. Downham, "The Good, the Bad, and the Ugly", 30, 31.
14. Radner, *Fragmentary Annals*, 95, 92.
15. Hermann and Edwards, *Landnámabók*, 55.

16. Hermann and Edwards, *Landnámabók*, 23.
17. Hermann and Edwards, *Landnámabók*, 117.
18. Hermann and Edwards, *Landnámabók*, 38.
19. Hermann and Edwards, *Landnámabók*, 55, 52.
20. Hermann and Edwards, *Landnámabók*, 126.
21. Durrenberger, "Anthropological Perspectives," 230.
22. Etchingham et al., *Norse-Gaelic Contacts*, 287.
23. Hermann and Edwards, *Landnámabók*, 56.
24. Turville-Petre, "*Liggja*," 52–58 and "Dreams," 48.
25. Turville-Petre, "*Liggja*," 52–58 and "Dreams," 48.
26. Hermann and Edwards, *Landnámabók*, 22, 35.
27. Magnusson, *Iceland Saga*, 236.
28. Scudder, "Egil's Saga," 40.
29. Scudder, "Egil's Saga, 41.
30. For example, the warriors in *Acallam na Senórach*: when St. Patrick's men saw them they "were seized with fear and horror at the sight of these enormous men, warriors of an earlier age." Dooley and Roe, *Tales of the Elders*, 5.
31. Scudder, "Egil's Saga", 59–63.
32. eDIL, s.v. 1 *brecc.*
33. Kunz, "Vínland Sagas," 636.
34. Kunz, "Vínland Sagas," 643.
35. Kunz, "Vínland Sagas," 644.
36. Kunz, "Vínland Sagas," 659.
37. Wawn, "Saga," 267.
38. Radner, *Fragmentary Annals*, 128.

5. NORSE HEATHENISM IN IRISH DYNASTIC NARRATIVES

1. Radner, *Fragmentary Annals*, xxvi.
2. Downham, "The Good, the Bad, and the Ugly," 27–28.
3. Todd, *Cogadh*.

4. Duffy, *Brian Boru*, 198. See also Casey, "Reconsideration."
5. Ó Corráin, "*Caithréim Chellacháin*," 5.
6. Radner, *Fragmentary Annals*, 92–93.
7. Radner, *Fragmentary Annals*, 132–33.
8. Radner, *Fragmentary Annals*, 134–35.
9. Todd, *Cogadh*, 40–41, emphasis added.
10. Todd, *Cogadh*, 48–49.
11. Todd, *Cogadh*, 52–53.
12. Todd, *Cogadh*, 152–53.
13. Todd, *Cogadh*, 202–23.
14. Bugge, *Chellacháin*, 7, 64.
15. Bugge, *Chellacháin*, 32, 90.
16. Bugge, *Chellacháin*, 40–41, 99.
17. Bugge, *Chellacháin*, 74–75.
18. Bugge, *Chellacháin*, 160–63.
19. Bugge, *Chellacháin*, 162–63.
20. Bugge, *Chellacháin*, 186–87.
21. Bugge, *Chellacháin*, 194–95.
22. Bugge, *Chellacháin*, 194–97.
23. Bugge, *Chellacháin*, 7, 64.
24. Bugge, *Chellacháin*, 8–9, 65–66.
25. Bugge, *Chellacháin*, 40, 99.
26. Radner, *Fragmentary Annals*, 98.
27. Bugge, *Chellacháin*, 71–72.
28. eDIL, s.v. *echtrann*: *adj.* strange, foreign; *as subst.* stranger, foreigner, alien; sometimes connoting enemy.
29. Duffy, *Brian Boru*, 201.
30. Todd, *Cogadh*, 48–49.
31. Todd, *Cogadh*, 114–15.
32. Murray, *Early Finn*, 22.
33. Todd, *Cogadh*, 174–75.
34. eDIL, s.v. *badb*.
35. Dillon, *Lebor* and Murray, *Early Finn*, 64.

36. eDIL, s.v. *síabraid*. Middle Irish *síabair*, from *síabriad* "distorts, transforms (for the worse); enchants, bewitches."
37. Todd, *Cogadh*, 201.
38. O'Rahilly, "Ir. Aobh," 3.
39. Duffy, *Brian Boru*, 189.
40. Duffy, *Brian Boru*, 66.
41. Todd, *Cogadh*, 196–99.
42. Radner, *Fragmentary Annals*, 102–3.
43. Carey, *Magic*, 17–18.
44. Macalister, *Memorial Slabs*, 132.
45. From Latin *certus*. eDIL *s.v.* 1 cert.
46. Dillon, *Lebor*, ix.
47. Radner, *Fragmentary Annals*, 108.
48. Radner, *Fragmentary Annals*, 102.

6. FOLKWAYS IN THE NORTH ATLANTIC

1. Ellis Davidson, *Lost Beliefs*, 81.
2. Bugge, *Studier over*.
3. Gísli, *Gaelic Influence*, 80.
4. Power, "An Óige," 243–44.
5. Almqvist, "Gaelic/Norse."
6. Wanner, *Snorri*, 8.
7. Ellis Davidson, *Lost Beliefs*, 81.
8. Power, "An Óige," 243.
10. Snorri, *Prose Edda*, 42.
11. Wanner, *Snorri*, 93.
12. Hermann and Edwards, *Landnámabók*, 6.
13. Agnar et al., "mtDNA."
14. Ellis Davidson, *Lost Beliefs*, 84.
15. Hermann and Edwards, *Landnámabók*, 44.
16. Power, "An Óige," 257.
17. Power, "An Óige," 239.

7. NORSE-GAELIC PAGANISM IN PRACTICE

1. McCone, "Werewolves," 18.
2. Todd, *Cogadh*, xcv, fn. 1.
3. Simek, *Dictionary*, 264.
4. Hutton, *Stations*, 218–22.

Bibliography

Icelandic names are patronymic (and, occasionally, matronymic). Both medieval and modern Icelanders are therefore alphabetized by their first name(s).

PRIMARY SOURCES

Annals of Ulster, from the Earliest Times to the Year 1541, 2nd ed. Vol. 1. Caislean Búrc le Éamonn de Búrca, 1998.

Broderick, George, trans. *Chronica Regum Manniæ et Insularum.* 3rd ed. Manx National Heritage, Douglas, 2004.

Bugge, Alexander, trans. and ed. *Caithreim Cellachain Caisil: The Victorious Career of Cellachan of Cashel, or, The Wars Between the Irishmen and the Norsemen in the Middle of the 10th Century.* Det Norske Historiske Kildeskriftfond, J. Chr. Gundersens Bogtrykkeri, Christiana, 1905.

Carey, John, trans. "The Adventure of Cormac [son of Art and] Grandson of Conn." In *The Celtic Heroic Age*, ed. John Koch. 4th ed. Celtic Studies Publications, 2005.

Cook, Robert, trans. and ed. *Njal's Saga.* Rev. ed. Penguin Classics. 2002.

Dillon, Myles, trans. and ed. *Lebor na Cert: The Book of Rights*. Irish Texts Society, 1962.

Dooley, Ann, and Harry Roe, trans. *Tales of the Elders of Ireland: A New Translation of* Acallam na Senórach. Oxford University Press, 1999.

Gantz, Jeffrey, trans. *Early Irish Myths and Sagas*. Penguin Books, 1981.

Grønlie, Siân, trans. *Íslendingabók, Kristni Saga: The Book of the Icelanders, The Story of the Conversion*. Vol. 18 of Viking Society for Northern Research Text Series, edited by Anthony Faulkes and Alison Finlay. University College London, 2006.

Hermann Pálsson and Paul Edwards, trans. *Landnámabók*. Vol. 1 of *University of Manitoba Icelandic Studies*. University of Manitoba Press, 1972.

Hermann Pálsson and Paul Edwards, trans. and eds. *Orkneyinga Saga: The History of the Earls of Orkney*. Reprint, Penguin Classics, 1981.

Kunz, Keneva, trans. "The Saga of the People of Laxardal (*Laxdæla Saga*)." In *The Sagas of Icelanders*, edited by Örnólfur Thorsson, 1997. Reprint, Penguin Books, 2001.

Kunz, Keneva, trans. "The Vinland Sagas (*Grœnlendinga saga* and *Eiríks saga rauða*)." In *The Sagas of Icelanders*, edited by Örnólfur Thorsson, 1997. Reprint, Penguin Books, 2001.

Lunde, Paul, and Caroline Stone, trans. *Ibn Fadlān and the Land of Darkness: Arab Travellers in the Far North*. Penguin Classics, 2005.

Mac Airt, Seán, trans. and ed. *The Annals of Inisfallen (MS Rawlinson B 503)*. Dublin Institute for Advanced Studies, 1988.

Macalister, R.A. Stewart. *The Memorial Slabs of Clonmacnoise, King's County*. University Press, 1909.

Radner, Joan N., trans. and ed. *Fragmentary Annals of Ireland*. Dublin Institute for Advanced Studies, 1978.

Scudder, Bernard, trans. "Egil's Saga (*Egils saga*)." In *The Sagas of Icelanders*, edited by Örnólfur Thorsson. 1997. Reprint, New York: Penguin Books, 2001.

Snorri Sturluson. *The Prose Edda: Tales from Norse Mythology*. Translated by Jean I. Young. University of California Press, 1954.

Terry, Patricia, trans. *Poems of the Elder Edda*. Rev. ed. University of Pennsylvania Press, 1990.

Todd, James Henthorn, trans. and ed. *Cogadh Gaedhel re Gallaibh: The War of the Gaedhil with the Gaill, or, The Invasions of Ireland by the Danes and Other Norsemen*. Longmans, Green, Reader, and Dyer, 1867.

Wawn, Andrew, trans. "The Saga of the People of Vatnsdala (*Vatnsdæla saga*)." In *The Sagas of Icelanders*, edited by Örnólfur Thorsson. 1997. Reprint, Penguin Books, 2001.

SECONDARY SOURCES

Abrams, Lesley. "Conversion and the Church in Viking-Age Ireland." In *The Viking Age: Ireland and the West*, edited by John Sheehan and Donnchadh Ó Corráin. Four Courts Press, 2010.

Abrams, Lesley. "The Conversion of the Scandinavians of Dublin." *Anglo-Norman Studies* 20, (1998): 1–29.

Agnar Helgason et al. "Estimating Scandinavian and Gaelic Ancestry in the Male Settlers of Iceland," *American Journal of Human Genetics* 67, no. 3 (2000): 697–717.

Agnar Helgason et al. "mtDNA and the Islands of the North Atlantic: Estimating the Proportions of Norse and Gaelic Ancestry." *American Journal of Human Genetics* 68, no. 3 (2001): 723–737.

Allan, W. E. D. *The Poet and the Spae-Wife: An Attempt to Reconstruct Al-Ghazal's Embassy to the Vikings*. Allen Figgis & Co., 1960.

Almqvist, Bo. "Gaelic/Norse Folklore Contacts: Some reflections on their scope and character." In *Irland und Europa im früheren Mittelalter: Bildung und Literatur,* edited by Próinséas Ní Chatháin and Michael Richter. Klett-Cotta, 1996.

Almqvist, Bo, and David Greene, eds. *Proceedings of the Seventh Viking Congress, Dublin 15–21 August 1973*. Royal Irish Academy, 1976.

Andersson, Theodore M. *The Problem of Icelandic Saga Origins*. Yale University Press, 1964.

Benedictow, Ole Jørgen. *The Medieval Demographic System of the Nordic Countries.* Middelalderforlaget, 1993.

Bibire, Paul. "North Sea Language Contacts in the Early Middle Ages: English and Norse." In *The North Sea World in the Middle Ages: Studies in the Cultural History of North-Western Europe*, edited by Thomas R. Liszka and Lorna E. M. Walker. Four Courts Press, 2001.

Bitel, Lisa M. *Land of Women: Tales of Sex & Gender from Early Ireland.* Cornell University Press, 1996.

Bitel, Lisa M. *Women in Early Medieval Europe, 400–1100.* Cambridge: University Press, 2002.

Brady, Lindy. "An Irish Sovereignty Motif in *Laxdæla Saga.*" *Scandinavian Studies* 88, no. 1 (2016): 60–76.

Bradley, John. "Toward a Definition of the Irish Monastic Town." In *Ædificia Nova: Studies in Honor of Rosemary Cramp*, edited by Catherine E. Karkov and Helen Damico. University of Michigan, 2008.

Brink, Stefan, and Neil Price, eds., *The Viking World.* Routledge, 2008.

Broderick, George. "Goidelic-Scandinavian Language Contact in the Place-Names of the Isle of Man." In *Language Contact in the Place-Names of Britain and Ireland*, edited by Paul Cavill and George Broderick. English Place-Name Society, 2007.

Broderick, George. *Placenames of the Isle of Man.* Vols. 1–7. Niemeyer, 1994–2005.

Bugge, Sophus. *Studier over de nordiske Gude- og Heltesagns Oprindelse.* University of Michigan Library Reprints, 1881.

Casey, Denis. "A Reconsideration of the Authorship and Transmission of *Cogadh Gáedhel re Gallaibh.*" *Proceedings of the Royal Irish Academy* 113C (2013): 139–161.

Carey, John. "*Lebor Gabála* and the Legendary History of Ireland." In *Medieval Celtic Literature and Society*, edited by Helen Fulton. Four Courts Press, 2005.

Carey, John. *Magic, Metallurgy & Imagination in Medieval Ireland: Three Studies.* Celtic Studies Publications, 2019.

Clarke, Howard B. "The Bloodied Eagle: The Vikings and the Development of Dublin, 841–1014." *The Irish Sword* 18, no. 71 (1991): 91–119.

Clarke, Howard B. "Unsung heroes: the Irish and Viking wars." In *Dublin in the Medieval World*, edited by J. Bradley, A. J. Fletcher, and A. Simms. Four Courts Press, 2009, 60–5.

Clarke, Howard B., and Ruth Johnson, eds. *The Vikings in Ireland and Beyond: Before and After the Battle of Clontarf.* Four Courts Press, 2015.

Clarke, Howard B., Sheila Dooley, and Ruth Johnson. *Dublin and the Viking World*. O'Brien Press, 2018.

Clunies Ross, Margaret, ed. *Poetry in fornaldarsögur: Skaldic Poetry of the Scandinavian Middle Ages*. Brepols, 2017.

Downham, Clare. "The career of Cearbhall of Osraighe." *Ossory, Laois & Leinster* 1 (2004): 1–18.

Downham, Clare. "Coastal Communities and Diaspora Identities in Viking Age Ireland." In *Maritime Societies of the Viking and Medieval World*, edited by James H. Barrett and Sarah Jane Gibbon. Routledge, 2016.

Downham, Clare. "The Good, the Bad and the Ugly: Portrayals of Vikings in 'The Fragmentary Annals of Ireland,'" *The Medieval Chronicle* 3 (2004): 28–40.

Downham, Clare. *Medieval Ireland.* Cambridge University Press, 2018.

Downham, Clare. "Religious and Cultural Boundaries between Vikings and Irish: The Evidence of Conversion." In *The March in the Islands of the Medieval West*, edited by Jenifer Ní Ghrádaigh and Emmett O'Byrne. Brill, 2012.

Downham, Clare. "Viking Identities in Ireland: It's not All Black and White." In *Medieval Dublin XI: Proceedings of the Friends of Medieval Dublin Symposium 2009*, edited by Seán Duffy. Four Courts Press, 2011.

Downham, Clare. *Viking Kings of Britain and Ireland: The Dynasty of Ívarr to A.D. 1020.* Dunedin Academic Press, 2007.

Downham, Clare. "The Viking Slave Trade: Entrepreneurs or Heathen Slavers?" *History Ireland*, 17, no. 3 (2009): 15–17.

duBois, Thomas A. "Juxtaposing *Cogadh Gáedel re Gallaib* with *Orkneyinga Saga*." *Oral Tradition* 26, no. 2 (2011): 267–96.

Duffy, Seán, "A Reconsideration of the Site of Dublin's Thing-mót." In *Above and Beyond: Essays in Memory of Leo Swan*, edited by Tom Condit and Christiaan Corlett. Wordwell, 2005.

Duffy, Seán. *Brian Boru and the Battle of Clontarf.* Gill & Macmillan, 2014.

Duffy, Seán. "Irishmen and Islesmen in the Kingdoms of Dublin and Man, 1052–1171." *Ériu*, 43 (1992): 93–133.

Duffy, Seán. "Ostmen, Irish and Welsh in the eleventh century." *Peritia* 9 (1995): 378–96.

Dumville, David N. "Old Dubliners and New Dubliners in Ireland and Britain: A Viking-Age Story." *Medieval Dublin VI: Proceedings of the Friends of Medieval Dublin Symposium* (2004): 78–93.

Durrenberger, E. Paul. "Anthropological Perspectives on the Commonwealth Period." In *The Anthropology of Iceland*, edited by E. Paul Durrenberger and Gísli Pálsson. University of Iowa, 1989.

eDIL 2019: *An Electronic Dictionary of the Irish Language*, based on the *Contributions to a Dictionary of the Irish Language*, Royal Irish Academy, 1913–1976. 2019.

Ellis Davidson, H. R. *Gods and Myths of Northern Europe.* Reprint, Pelican, 1977.

Ellis Davidson, H. R. *The Lost Beliefs of Northern Europe.* Routledge, 1993.

Etchingham, Colmán. "Names for the Vikings in Irish Annals." In *Celtic-Norse Relations in the Irish Sea in the Middle Ages 800–1200*, edited by Jón Viðar Sigurðsson and Timothy Bolton. Brill, 2014.

Etchingham, Colmán. "The Location of Historical *Laithlinn/Lochlainn*: Scotland or Scandinavia?" In *Studia Celtica Upsaliensia: Proceedings of a Symposium of the Societas Celtologica Nordica*, edited by M. Ó Flaithearta. Uppsala, 2004.

Etchingham, Colmán, Jón Viðar Sigurðsson, Máire Ní Mhaonaigh, and Elizabeth Ashman Rowe. *Norse-Gaelic Contacts in a Viking World: Studies in the Literature and History of Norway, Iceland, Ireland, and the Isle of Man.* Vol. 29 of *Medieval Texts and Cultures of Northern Europe.* Brepols, 2019.

Fellows-Jensen, Gillian. "Scandinavian Settlement in the Isle of Man and

Northwest England: The Place-Name Evidence." In *The Viking Age in the Isle of Man: Selected Papers from the Ninth Viking Congress, Isle of Man 4–14 July 1981*, edited by Christine E. Fell et al. Viking Society for Northern Research, University College London, 1983.

Fellows-Jenson, Gillian. "Viking Settlement in the Northern and Western Isles: The Place-Name Evidence as Seen from Denmark and the Danelaw." In *Northern and Western Isles in the Viking World: Continuity and Change, for the Bicentenary of the National Museum of Antiquities of Scotland, 1781–1981*, edited by Alexander Fenton and Hermann Pálsson. John Donald, 1984.

Foster, R. F., ed. *The Oxford Illustrated History of Ireland*. Oxford University Press, 2001.

Frank, Roberta. "*Beowulf* and Sutton Hoo: The odd couple." In *The Archaeology of Anglo-Saxon England*, edited by Catherine E. Karkov, New York, 1999, 317–38.

Frank, Roberta. "The Boar on the Helmet." In *Ædificia Nova: Studies in Honor of Rosemary Cramp*, edited by Catherine E. Karkov and Helen Damico. University of Michigan, 2008.

Gammeltoft, Peder. "Scandinavian-Gaelic Contacts: Can Place-Names and Place-Name Elements Be Used as a Source for Contact-Linguistic Research?" *NOWELE North-Western European Language Evolution* 44, no. 1 (2004): 51–90.

Gibbons, Michael. "The *Longphort* Phenomenon in Early Christian and Viking Ireland." *History Ireland* 12, no. 3 (2004): 19–23.

Gibson, D. Blair. *From Chiefdom to State in Early Ireland.* Cambridge University Press, 2012.

Gísli Sigurðsson. "The Saga Map of Ireland and the British Isles." In *Clerics, Vikings, and High-Kings*, edited by Elmer Purcell, et al. Four Courts Press, 2015.

Gísli Sigurðsson. *Gaelic Influence in Iceland: Historical and Literary Contacts, A Survey of Research.* 2nd ed. University of Iceland Press, 2000.

Gísli Sigurðsson. "*Njáls saga* and Its Listeners' Assumed Knowledge: Applying Notions of Mediality to a Medieval Text." In *RE:Writing:*

Medial Perspectives on textual Culture in the Icelandic Middle Ages, edited by Kate Heslop and Jürd Glauser. Chronos Verlag, 2018.

Goedheer, Albertus Johannes. *Irish and Norse Traditions About the Battle of Clontarf.* H. D. Tjeenk Willink & Zoon N. V., 1938.

Griffiths, David. *Vikings of the Irish Sea: Conflict and Assimilation AD 790–1050.* History Press, 2010.

Heng, Geraldine. *The Invention of Race in the European Middle Ages.* Cambridge University Press, 2018.

Herbert, Máire. "Sea-divided Gaels? Constructing Relationships Between Irish and Scots c. 800–1169." In *Britain and Ireland, 900–1300: Insular Responses to Medieval European Change*, edited by Brendan Smith. Cambridge University Press, 1999.

Holinshed, Raphael. *Holinshed's Chronicles England, Scotland, and Ireland.* Edited by Vernon F. Snow. AMS, 1965.

Holm, Poul. "The Naval Power of Norse Dublin." In *Clerics, Vikings, and High-Kings*, edited by Emer Purcell et al. Four Courts Press, 2015.

Holm, Poul. "Viking Dublin and the City-State Concept: Parameters and Significance of the Hiberno-Norse Settlement." In *A Comparative Study of Thirty City-state Cultures*, edited by Mogens Herman Hansen. 2000.

Hudson, Benjamin. "The Changing Economy of the Irish Sea Province." In *Britain and Ireland, 900–1300: Insular Responses to Medieval European Change,* edited by Brendan Smith. Cambridge University Press, 1999.

Hudson, Benjamin. *Irish Sea Studies 900–1200.* Dublin, Four Courts Press, 2006.

Hudson, Benjamin. "Lothlind. In McAlister, Vicky, and Terry Barry, eds. *Space and Settlement in Medieval Ireland,* Four Courts Press, Dublin, 2015, pp. 1-14.

Hudson, Benjamin. *Viking Pirates and Christian Princes: Dynasty, Religion, and Empire in the North Atlantic.* Oxford University Press, 2005.

Hughes, A. J., and R. Hannan. *The place-names of Northern Ireland*, vol. 2. QUB Institute of Irish Studies, 1992.

Humphrey, Ann C. *The Memory of the Norse in Ireland in Middle Irish*

Dynastic Narratives, Trinity College Dublin, School of Histories & Humanities, History, 2023. Trinity College Dublin website.

Hutton, Ronald. *The Stations of the Sun: A History of the Ritual Year in Britain*. Oxford University Press, 1996.

Jesch, Judith. *Women in the Viking Age.* Boydell Press, 1991.

Jochens, Jenny. *Women in Old Norse Society.* Cornell University Press, 1995.

Johnston, Elva. *Literacy and Identity in Early Medieval Ireland.* Boydell Press, Boydell & Brewer, 2013.

Jóhanna Katrín Friðriksdóttir. *Women in Old Norse Literature: Bodies, Words, and Power.* Palgrave Macmillan, 2013.

Jón Viðar Sigurðsson and Timothy Bolton, eds. *Celtic-Norse Relations in the Irish Sea in the Middle Ages 800–1200.* Brill, 2014.

Jón Jóhannesson. *A History of the Old Icelandic Commonwealth: Íslendinga Saga.* Translated by Haraldur Bessason. Vol. 2 of *University of Manitoba Icelandic Studies*, 1974. Reprint. University of Manitoba Press, 2006.

Jónas Kristánsson. "Ireland and the Irish in Icelandic Tradition." In *Ireland and Scandinavia in the Early Viking Age*, edited by Howard B. Clarke, Máire Ní Mhaonaigh, and Raghnall Ó Floinn. Four Courts Press, 1998.

Kruse, Arne. "The Norway to Be: *Laithlind* and Avaldsnes." In *Traversing the Inner Seas: Contacts and Continuity in and around Scotland, the Hebrides, and the North of Ireland*, edited by Christian Coojimans. Scottish Society for Northern Studies, 2017.

Lenihan, Eddie, and Carolyn Eve Green. *Meeting the Other Crowd.* Tarcher, 2003.

Lyall, Sarah. "Building in Iceland? Better Clear It with the Elves First." *New York Times*, July 13, 2005.

MacCotter, Paul. *Medieval Ireland: Territorial, Political and Economic Divisions.* Four Courts Press, 2008.

MacDonald, Donald A. "The Vikings in Gaelic Oral Tradition." In *Northern and Western Isles in the Viking World: Continuity and Change, for the Bicentenary of the National Museum of Antiquities of Scotland, 1781–1981*, edited by Alexander Fenton and Hermann Pálsson. John Donald, 1984.

Mac Eoin, Gearóid. "The Original Name of the Viking Settlement at

Limerick." In *Northern Lights: Following Folklore in North-West Europe. Essays in Honour of Bo Almqvist*, edited by Séamas Ó Catháin et al. University College Dublin, 2001.

Macniven, Alan. *The Vikings in Islay: The Place of Names in Hebridean Settlement History*. John Donald, Birlinn, 2015.

Magnusson, Magnus. *Iceland Saga*. Revised edition, Tempus, 2005.

Marstrander, Carl J. S. *Bidrag til del Norske sprogs historie i Irland*. J. Dybwad, Kristiana, 1915.

McAlister, Deirdre. "Childhood in Viking and Hiberno-Scandinavian Dublin, 800–1100." In *Everyday Life in Viking-Age Towns: Social Approaches to Towns in England and Ireland, c. 800–1100*, edited by D. M. Hadley and Letty ten Harkel. Oxbow Books, 2013.

McCone, Kim R. "Werewolves, Cyclopes, *Díberga* and *Fíanna*: Juvenile Delinquency in Early Ireland." *Cambridge Medieval Celtic Studies* 12 (Winter 1986): 1–22.

McDonald, R. Andrew. "Man, Ireland, and England: the English Conquest of Ireland and Dublin-Manx Relations." In *Medieval Dublin VIII: Proceedings of the Friends of Medieval Dublin Symposium 2006*, edited by Seán Duffy. Four Courts Press, 2008.

McDonald, R. Andrew. *Manx Kingship in Its Irish Sea Setting, 1187–1229: King Rognvaldr and the Crovan Dynasty*. Four Courts Press, 2007.

McDonald, R. Andrew. *The Sea Kings: The Late Norse Kingdoms of Man and the Isles, c. 1066–1275*. Birlinn, 2019.

McDonald, Roderick W. "Dynamics of Identity: Norse Loanword-borrowers in Ireland and Scotland, and Linguistic Evidence of Urbanization." *Eolas: The Journal of the American Society of Irish Medieval Studies* 11 (2018): 2–31.

McDonald, Roderick W. "Vikings in the Hebridean Economy: Methodology and Gaelic Language Evidence of Scandinavian Influence." *Zeitschrift für celtische Philologie* 62, no. 1, 2015, 97–182.

Moore, A. W. *The Folk-Lore of the Isle of Man, Being an Account of its Myths, Legends, Superstitions, Customs & Proverbs*. 1891. Facsimile reprint, Llanerch, 1994.

Murray, Kevin. *The Early Finn Cycle.* Fourt Courts Press, 2017.

Ní Chonaill, Brónagh. "Flying a Kite with the Children of Hiberno-Norse Dublin: A Tentative Social Exploration." In *Ireland and Scandinavia in the Early Viking Age,* edited by Howard B. Clarke, Máire Ní Mhaonaigh, and Raghnall Ó Floinn. Four Courts Press, 1998.

Ní Mhaonaigh, Máire. *Brian Boru: Ireland's Greatest King?* Tempus Publishing, 2006.

Ní Mhaonaigh, Máire. "Friend and Foe: Vikings in Ninth- and Tenth-Century Irish Literature." In *Ireland and Scandinavia in the Early Viking Age,* edited by Howard B. Clarke, Máire Ní Mhaonaigh, and Raghnall Ó Floinn. Four Courts Press, 1998.

Ní Mhaonaigh, Máire. "Literary *Lochlann.*" In *Cànan & Cultar / Language & Culture: Rannsachadh na Gàidhlig 3,* edited by Wilson McLeod, James E. Fraser, and Anja Gunderloch. Dunedin Academic Press, 2006.

Ó Corráin, Donnchadh. "*Caithréim Chellacháin Chaisil*: History or Propaganda?" *Eriú* 25 (1974): 1–69.

Ó Corráin, Donnchadh. "Old Norse and Medieval Irish: Bilingualism in Viking-Age Dublin." In *Ireland and Scandinavia in the Early Viking Age,* edited by Howard B. Clarke, Máire Ní Mhaonaigh, and Raghnall Ó Floinn. Four Courts Press, 1998.

Ó Corráin, Donnchadh. "The Vikings in Scotland and Ireland in the Ninth Century." *Peritia* 12 (1998): 296–338.

Ó Cróinín, Dáibhí. *Early Medieval Ireland, 400–1200.* Longman, 1995.

Ó Cróinín, Dáibhí. *A New History of Ireland: Prehistoric and Early Ireland.* Clarendon Press, 2008.

O'Leary, Philip. "The Honour of Women in Early Irish Literature," *Ériu* 38 (1987): 27–44.

O'Rahilly, T. F. "Ir. Aobh, Aoibheall, Etc. W. Ufel, Uwel. Gaul. Esus." *Ériu* 14 (1946): 1–6.

Orri Vésteinsson. "Ethnicity and Class in Settlement-Period Iceland." In *Dublin in the Medieval World,* edited by J. Bradley, A. J. Fletcher, and A. Simms. Four Courts Press, 2009.

Power, Rosemary. "'*An Óige, an Saol agus an Bas,' Feis Tighe Chonáin* and 'Þorr's Visit to Utgarða-Loki.'" *Béaloideas* 53 (1985): 217–94.

Power, Rosemary. "Meeting in Norway: Norse-Gaelic Relations in the Kingdom of Man and the Isles, 1090–1270." *Saga-Book* 29 (2005): 5–66.

Price, Neil S. *The Viking Way: Magic and Mind in Late Iron Age Scandinavia*. 2nd ed. Oxbow, 2019.

Sayers, William. "Birds and Brains of Forgetfulness: Old Norse *óminnis hegri*, Old Irish *inchinn dermait*." *Journal of Indo-European Studies* 43, no. 3–4 (2015): 393–422.

Sayers, William. "Clontarf, and the Irish Destinies of Sigurðr Digri, Earl of Orkney, and Þorsteinn Síðu-Hallsson." *Scandinavian Studies* 63, no. 2 (Spring 1991): 164–86.

Sayers, William. "The Etymology and Semantics of Old Norse *Knǫrr* 'cargo ship': The Irish and English Evidence." *Scandinavian Studies* 68, no. 3 (1996): 279–90.

Sayers, William."'Vífill—Captive Gael, Freeman Settler, Icelandic Forbear." *Ainm* 6 (1994–95): 46–55.

Sheehan, Sarah, and Ann Dooley, eds. *Constructing Gender in Medieval Ireland*. Palgrave MacMillan, 2013.

Simek, Rudolf. *A Dictionary of Northern Mythology*. Boydell and Brewer, 1996.

Simpson, Linzi. "A Viking Warrior Grave from Dublin." In *The Vikings in Ireland and Beyond*, edited by Howard B. Clarke and Ruth Johnson. Four Courts Press, 2015.

Simpson, Linzi. "Fifty Years A-Digging: A Synthesis of Medieval Archaeological Investigations in Dublin City and Suburbs." In *Medieval Dublin XI: Proceedings of the Friends of Medieval Dublin Symposium 2009*, edited by Seán Duffy. Four Courts Press, 2011.

Simpson, Linzi. "The First Phase of Viking Activity in Ireland: Archaeological Evidence from Dublin." In *Dublin in the Medieval World*, edited by J. Bradley, A. J. Fletcher, and A. Simms. Four Courts Press, 2009.

Skre, Daugfinn. "From Kaupang and Avaldsnes to the Irish Sea." In *Clerics, Vikings, and High-Kings*, edited by Emer Purcell, et al. Four Courts Press, 2015.

Sonne, Lasse C. A. "The Northification of the Pagan Past in Old Norse Literature." In *Historical and Intellectual Culture in the Long Twelfth Century: The Scandinavian Connection*, edited by Mia Münster-Swendsen, Thomas K. Heebøll-Holm, and Sigbjørn Olsen Sønnesyn. Durham Publications in Medieval and Renaissance Studies, 2016.

Steinforth, Dirk H. "Early Vikings in the Isle of Man: Old Paradigms and New Perspectives." *Viking and Medieval Scandinavia* 11 (2015): 203–29.

Steinforth, Dirk H. "'That Stepping-Stone in the Middle of the Irish Sea': The Dublin Vikings and the Isle of Man in the Late Ninth Century." *The Journal of Irish Archaeology* 27 (2018): 81–97.

Suppe, F. "'Irish' Welshmen: The Social and Cultural Connotations of the Nickname Gwyddel in Medieval Wales." *Cambrian Medieval Celtic Studies* 78 (2019): 71–99.

Swift, Catherine. "Celtic Berserkers and Feeble Steersmen: Hiberno-Scandinavian Military Culture in Middle Irish Literature." In *The Vikings in Ireland and Beyond*, edited by Howard B. Clarke and Ruth Johnson. Four Courts Press, 2015. Boydell & Brewer, 1996.

Turville-Petre, Gabriel. "Dreams in Icelandic Tradition." In *Nine Norse Studies*, Vol. 5 of Viking Society for Northern Research. Western Printing Services, 1972.

Turville-Petre, Gabriel. "*Liggja Fylgjur Þínar Til Íslands*." In *Nine Norse Studies*, Vol. 5 of Viking Society for Northern Research. Western Printing Services, 1972.

Turville-Petre, Gabriel. "The Cult of Óðinn in Iceland." In *Nine Norse Studies*, Vol. 5 of Viking Society for Northern Research. Western Printing Services, 1972.

Valante, Mary. *The Vikings in Ireland: Settlement, Trade and Urbanization*. Four Courts Press, 2008.

Valante, Mary. "Viking Kings and Irish Fleets During Dublin's Viking Age." In *Ireland and Scandinavia in the Early Viking Age*, edited by Howard

B. Clarke, Máire Ní Mhaonaigh, and Raghnall Ó Floinn. Four Courts Press, 1998.

Vohra, P. "One of us? Negotiating Multiple Legal Identities Across the Viking Diaspora." *Ethnic and Racial Studies* 39, no. 2 (2016): 204–222.

Wadden, Patrick. "Dál Riata *c.* 1000: Genealogies and Irish Sea Politics." *The Scottish Historical Review* 95, pt. 2, no. 241 (October 2016): 164–181.

Wadden, Patrick. "Theories of National Identity in Early Medieval Ireland." PhD diss., Oxford University, 2012.

Wallace, Patrick F. "Irish Archaeology and the Recognition of Ethnic Difference in Viking Dublin." In *Evaluating Multiple Narratives: Beyond Nationalist, Colonialist, Imperialist Archaeologies,* edited by Junko Habu, Clare Fawcett, and John M. Matsunaga. Springer: 2008.

Wallace, Patrick F. "'Meagre lead': The Ubiquity of Lead in Hiberno-Scandinavian Dublin.' In *Clerics, Vikings, and High-Kings,* edited by Emer Purcell et al. Four Courts Press, 2015.

Wanner, Kevin J. *Snorri Sturluson and the Edda: The Conversion of Cultural Capital in Scandinavia.* University of Toronto Press, 2008.

Wamers, Egon. "Insular Finds in Viking Age Scandinavia." In *Ireland and Scandinavia in the Early Viking Age,* edited by Howard B. Clarke, Máire Ní Mhaonaigh, and Raghnall Ó Floinn. Four Courts Press, 1998.

Wilson, David. "The Chronology of the Viking Age in the Isle of Man.' *Proceedings of the Isle of Man Natural History and Antiquarian Society* 10, no. 4 (1998): 359–72.

Wilson, David. *The Vikings in the Isle of Man.* Aarhus University Press, 2008.

Woolf, Alex. *From Pictland to Alba, 789–1070.* Vol. 2 of *The New Edinburgh History of Scotland.* Edinburgh University Press, 2007.

Zoëga, Geir T. *A Concise Dictionary of Old Icelandic.* 1910. Reprint, Dover Publications, 2004.

Index